DECORATING FOR
CHRISTMAS

70 Themed Craft Projects to Decorate Your Home

C A R O L Y N   S C H U L Z

David & Charles

DEDICATION

I dedicate this book to my devoted father Bernard, who taught me how to observe,
to my generous mother Wanda, who taught me the love of creating with my hands,
and to my patient husband Tony who has lived with Christmas every day
for the past four years. Their constant love and support has made all this possible.

A DAVID & CHARLES BOOK

First published in the UK in 1996
Reprinted in 1997

A catalogue record for this book is available from the British Library.

ISBN 0 7153 0187 X

Project Editor: Heather Dewhurst
Photography by Caroline Arber
Styling by Tina Guillory
Illustrations by Chris King
Book design by Anita Ruddell
Printed in Great Britain by Butler & Tanner Ltd
for David & Charles
Brunel House   Newton Abbot   Devon

Contents

Introduction

$\mathcal{W}$ITH THE INCREASING AMOUNT of leisure time available to us today, more and more people are becoming involved in the 'do-it-yourself' trend. In addition to pursuing sports and other traditional hobbies, we are spending more time improving our domestic environment. We want to make our homes more attractive as well as more comfortable.

Within the sphere of home decor it has become more and more fashionable to use a theme incorporating colour and design. With its appeal to the eye, it becomes quite natural to extend this idea of co-ordinating design into the special decoration of our homes which takes place once a year at Christmas.

In this book I have singled out five distinctive decorating themes for the festive season, in addition to alternative colour themes – Tartan, Toyland, Scandinavian, Victorian and Country - and have given a host of ideas for decorating your tree, table and home within each particular theme. For example, the Tartan theme explores the use of perfectly ruched bows in its decorations, while the Toyland theme will delight all children with its sweetie garland, Santa stocking (opposite) and teddy bear tree decorations. The Scandinavian theme focuses on traditional Norwegian and Danish festive decorations, such as woven hearts and sheaves of wheat, while the Victorian theme shows what you can make with a profusion of lace, ribbons and pearls. Finally, the Country theme takes its inspiration from nature and shows how to make decorations for the tree, room and table from natural ingredients.

When you decide you want to choose a theme, you don't need to have a clean or blank canvas on which to start working. In other words, don't rush to the loft or garage and give away all your precious festive ornaments you have collected over the years. Look at what ornaments you have and put those which have special meaning to one side. Look carefully at the special ornaments you have kept. What is it that makes them special? Do some of them represent special events, occasions or people in your life or the lives of your family? You can hang these ornaments at strategic positions all over your tree, no matter what theme you follow. Let them personalize your tree and remind you of the special thoughts that go with them.

Despite the increased commercialism of the Christmas season, it is still a very special time of year. To each of us it has a different meaning and we can express this through the decorations that we use throughout the home. Themes can be more than co-ordinating colours, textures and shapes. They can express peace and joy or fun and laughter, and I believe that, through a theme, you can share with others a little of yourself and your personality. I hope this book will give you the confidence to experiment with making and using themed Christmas decorations, and help you to create a unique and special look in your home.

CHAPTER 1

Decorating the Christmas Tree
A Step-by-Step Guide

DECORATING THE CHRISTMAS TREE can be one of the most pleasurable experiences of the holiday preparations, providing the creator with a true sense of achievement. Often we are harassed with too much to do and too little time in which to do it. With the suggestions in this step-by-step guide, I hope to provide you with the means of creating your perfect Christmas tree, as well as making it an enjoyable and enduring tradition.

Mental attitude is very important. Don't feel that you have to decorate the entire tree in one session. There is nothing worse than having the whole family standing around, with their favourite ornaments in hand, impatiently waiting for you to wire on the lights or sling on the garland. In this situation, everyone ends up frustrated and reality often fails to resemble the creation envisaged.

I prefer to trim the tree by working through the preliminary basic stages over a few days, usually after the children have gone to bed. Each morning they eagerly look to see how the design is developing. They know that I am doing the tedious steps which form the background for the fun to come. Usually the weekend before Christmas we have a tree-trimming party when the whole family joins in to put their ornaments into position.

I start by positioning the tree in its stand or container for a couple of days to give the branches a chance to settle. If you are using an artificial tree you will need to spread out the branches. A little steam can help the artificial silk trees look more fresh and lively.

If electric lights are used, these must be placed into position before progressing onto any other stages. This is one of the most important basics and the one I like the least. For this reason I have tried scrimping on the number of lights and even bribed other members of the family to put them up. The fact is, nothing can enhance the design of your tree more than properly placed lights, so take your time, and grin and bear it!

Draping the garland and attaching the bows follows the placement of lights. At the completion of each stage your tree will be dressed. If you prefer, or sufficient time is not available to continue, this in itself will provide you with a decorated tree, effective in the simplicity of its design.

STEP 1
LIGHTS

There are many types of lights available today. There are coloured lights and lights which flash; there are musical lights and lights in various shapes, such as candles and figures. My favourites are the small crystal lights which are used only as a source of lighting up and emphasizing the ornaments on the tree.

Lighting is very important on a Christmas tree. The more light there is available, the more effective your tree will look. Miniature lights placed on the tree will brighten up the space where they are placed, adding depth as well as sparkle. Spotlights emphasize the shape of the tree as well as providing a surface glow to the other tree decorations.

I like to use lots of lights and collect inexpensive strands of small plain crystal lights. I start at the top of the tree and work down with the lights plugged in so I can see where they are being placed. With more than one string of lights I find it easier to work down one section of the tree for each strand. Choose lights with green cord for green trees; attach the cord to the tree branches with 4in (10cm) pieces of green florist's wire to hide the cord as much as possible. Work along a branch from the trunk out to the tip and back again.

STEP 2

GARLANDS

The garland ties together the various segments of the decorated tree. There are many things which can be used as a tree garland; a few ideas are illustrated on page 11, but why not use your imagination to create an original garland for your chosen theme?

Garlands can be draped on the tree in several different ways. The more traditional way, as seen on the Victorian tree, is the swag pattern which is more formal. There are several variations to the swag, which can include hanging two or three strands at a time or criss-crossing the swags over each other from both directions. On the Scandinavian tree I have strung the flag garlands in vertical lines down the tree. An alternative you could consider is running twisted ribbon from the top of the tree to the base.

Whichever garland or method of draping the Christmas tree you choose, it is best to start at the back of the top of the tree and work down the branches. Use green florist's wire to attach the garland to the branches. Step back from the tree frequently as you are working to survey the effect of the garland. Then, if necessary, any alterations can be made before progressing too far.

STEP 3
BOWS

Decorative ribbon bows can add the finishing touch to your Christmas tree just as they do to gift-wrapped parcels. I like to use bows to accent the swag design of the tree garland, making it appear as if the bows are holding the swag to the branches. Today we are quite spoilt for choice with so many different ribbons readily available which create lovely full bows that hold their shape easily. Another of my personal favourites is wire-edged ribbon which can be shaped to perfection (see the samples on page 11).

STEP 4
ORNAMENTS

It is at this stage of tree decoration when the true character of the tree takes shape. Within the framework of your theme, the repetition of certain ornaments will allow the theme to become discernible.

Hang one type of ornament at a time, such as various-sized miniature parcels, scattering them around the branches. Repeat with other decorations, one type at a time. Hang larger ornaments towards the bottom of the tree, and graduate the sizes up towards the top where you can place smaller ones.

Making Bows

Many people shy away from making their own bows, thinking that they are too difficult, or perhaps they have tried unsuccessfully. I have chosen three of the easiest bows, using techniques I find foolproof. Try them – you will be pleasantly surprised!

SINGLE BOW

Cut two strips of the chosen material (ribbon, lace, fabric, etc) measuring 13in (32.5cm) and 18in (45cm) long respectively, and 1½in (4cm) wide. Fold the shorter strip in half to find the centre. Scrunch the strip along this central line and hold this with one hand while forming loops with each of the cut ends of the paper strips with the other hand. Overlap the loops by ½–1in (12mm–2.5cm). Wrap wire around the scrunched centre to secure.

Take the longer strip and place the centre over the middle of the front of the bow loops already formed. Wrap this strip around to the back of the bow and tie the ends together in a knot, pulling tightly to hold. This forms the bow tails. Cut a V-notch in the bow tails.

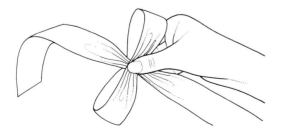

DOUBLE BOW

Cut two strips of material as for the single bow, then cut a third strip 11in (27.5cm) long. Make separate bow loops using the 13in (32.5cm) and the 11in (27.5cm) strips, as for the single bow. Place the small set of loops over the larger set of loops, holding them together in the centre. Tie the longest strip of material around both sets of loops and knot at the back to make the bow tails for the double bow. Cut a V-shaped notch in the bow tails.

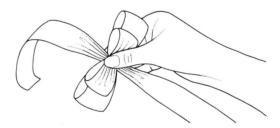

FLUFFY DOUBLE-LOOP BOW

Make two sets of loops as for the double bow. Wire each set together side by side. Stack the small loops over the large loops and tie them together with an 18in (45cm) strip of ribbon. Fluff out, and cut a V-notch in the bow tails.

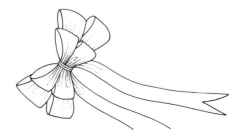

Single bows (top), double bows (centre), fluffy double-loop bows (below) and a selection of tree garlands

CHAPTER 2

Colour Themes

As in home decoration, colour is the most popular theme used in Christmas tree design. A colour theme can mean one, two, three or a multitude of colours. The traditional Christmas colours of bright red and green can be mixed with each other or individually with other colours to create many different colour themes with varying effects. Often gold or silver are combined with other colours, creating an even wider selection of colour themes.

Colour need not be the exclusive element of any Christmas decorating theme. As you will see in the chapters that follow, colour can very much complement another theme. Colour can also make a difference in how a theme is perceived. For example, it would be very hard to produce a warm, natural country Christmas theme using varying blues and silvers. However, with the use of rustic reds and natural wheaten tones, one can obtain the warm cosy setting that cool blues and glitzy silvers never could.

When choosing a successful colour theme for home decoration at Christmas, it is wise to take into consideration the existing colour scheme and room decor. This does not mean that the tree and room decorations should be exactly the same as those used in the room decor. It does mean, however, that it can be important to find colour combinations that will blend in with the colours and setting that already exist. The final result should complement the total look.

In this chapter I have chosen two colour combinations, and I have duplicated the tree and home decorations in each of these combinations. Each of the two themes has gold as the prominent colour, which is then combined

with a secondary colour to produce devastatingly different results. Notice the difference that the choice of second colour makes.

The white and gold combination of colours lends itself very well to many room settings and colour schemes, creating a subtle elegance. The combination of silver and white creates a very similar effect. Although not necessary, you could add a third colour, possibly a colour chosen from the room decor (such as burgundy, pink, navy or peach, etc), to accent the colour scheme of the room. By introducing a third colour, you can very easily create a new theme with a different effect, which could make it blend even more closely with the room setting.

Because red is considered a Christmas colour, one can get away with introducing it into most room settings. However, the red and gold colour combination is not as versatile when it comes to introducing other accent colours. Being an aggressive colour, red can have an overpowering effect in a room setting. However, by carefully manipulating the amount of red decoration that is mixed in with the gold, you can control whether your Christmas tree reflects a rich festive warmth or an over-strong boldness.

WHITE/GOLD TREE

For my first theme I have chosen to combine gold with a pearl white for subtle elegance. The pearl softens the glitter of the gold to make it more subdued.

Miniature crystal lights reflect on the sequinned ornaments to produce a soft glow on this exquisite colour combination. Fluffy double bows formed out of paper ribbon hold up double swags of thick gold cord. The tree branches are loaded with glistening ornaments, from miniature crackers, gemstone baubles and fashionable angels to small gift parcels. Crowning it all is a glorious pearl-studded star.

Pincraft ornaments (see page 16)

RED/GOLD TREE

For this colour theme I have combined red with gold to achieve bold brilliant colour. This tree is identical to my white and gold tree, except for the exchange of red for white. Sequinned ornaments glisten in reflected light from the miniature crystal lights. The multi-faceted gemstones reflect the red and gold colours from the surrounding ornaments, making the whole tree shimmer with opulent extravagance. Rich red and gold clothballs hang alongside elegant accordian angels nestling in the greenery. The branches of the tree are laden with small gift boxes and miniature crackers which are decorated with a profusion of curls. The tree-top star is the perfect way to finish this enticing vision of Christmas warmth and cheer.

WHITE AND GOLD TREE

RED AND GOLD TREE

Tree Decorations

The trees in this chapter are decorated with sparkling pincraft ornaments, all of which are very easy to make. In addition, accordian angels sit among fluffy double-loop bows made from gold paper ribbon. Clothballs, crackers and gemstone ornaments complete the colourful theme.

PINCRAFT ORNAMENTS
GENERAL INSTRUCTIONS

These general instructions will be particularly useful to first time pincrafters. By using these basic techniques, one can design original creations using a range of materials and colour combinations.

1 Divide each polystyrene shape into four equal sections using a pencil. Sections should run up and down the length of the shape.

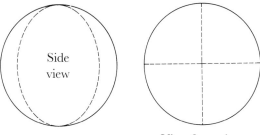

Side view

View from above

2 Cover the pencil lines with ribbon, lace or braid, according to the chosen design. Start by fixing one cut end of the ribbon to the top of the shape with a short pin. Run the ribbon down the side of the shape, around the bottom and back up to the top (dividing the shape in half). Overlap the ribbon slightly and fix it with a short pin. Cut the ribbon and repeat, at right angles, over the remaining pencil line, to make four equal sections. Measure the blank spaces between the ribbon to ensure they are equal. The ribbon should be wound tightly so that it does not slip off.

3 Fill in the blank spaces between the ribbon with pearls, sequins or beads on short pins, as directed for a particular design. There are different ways in which sequin units will be used and described. Listed below are terms you may come across. Note that, unless otherwise stated, sequins are all ¼in (6mm) cup:

Bead and sequin unit – 'cup up': This means you thread onto a short pin a bead (if required) then a concave cup sequin.

Bead and sequin unit – 'cup down': This means you thread onto a short pin a bead (if required) then a convex cup sequin.

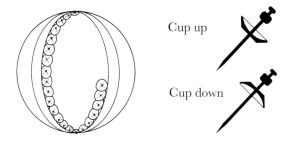

Cup up

Cup down

Starting at the bottom of one section, run a row of the sequin units up the edge of the ribbon to the top. Run another row of units

up the edge of the ribbon on the other side. Fill in the space between with rows of units.

4 To make ribbon loops at the top of the ornament, place two long pins so that they are firmly fixed, yet protruding, one-third of the

Red and gold tree-top star

way down from the top of the shape in the centre of two opposite sections. These are guide pins and should be removed after the

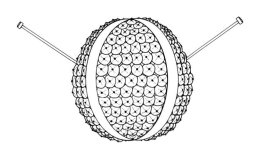

ribbon loops are completed. Fix one cut end of the ribbon to the centre top of the shape. Keep the ribbon flat (do not twist it). Wind it clockwise around one guide pin and back to the centre. Continue winding, this time anti-clockwise around the other guide pin. Check to see that this figure-of-eight set of loops is of equal length and fullness on both sides. Use short pins to fix into place.

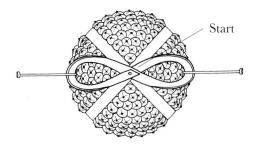

Start

5 Make another set of loops, directly over the previous set, without cutting the ribbon. Replace the guide pins ¼ in (6mm) closer to the top of the shape. Form a second set of loops over the first ones, except a little shorter.

6 Form a set of loops at right angles over the remaining two sections of the shape, this time cutting the ribbon. Start with step 4, forming loops around guide pins placed in the other two sections.

7 Make a hanging loop by forming a large loop with 6–8in (15–20cm) ribbon. Overlap the two cut ends and fix them to the centre top of the ornament using short pins.

8 Decorate the ornament as desired.

TREE-TOP STAR

MATERIALS

The materials given are for a white and gold star. The colours to be used for the red and gold star are given in brackets.

Moulded polystyrene star, 8in (20cm) in diameter
Gold (red) acrylic paint
Paintbrush
52in (1.3m) gold braid
Scissors
1,350 brass pins, 4 x .55mm
1,250 white (gold) pearl beads, ⅛ in (3mm)
36 white (gold or red) pearlized teardrop hat pins or corsage pins, 2in (5cm) long
6 gold filigree cones, 1½ in (4cm) long
Tacky glue
Florist's wire

1 Paint the star both front and back with three coats of acrylic paint.

2 Starting at the centre of one side of the star, wrap gold braid around the star, over two opposite points and back to the centre. Cut the braid and repeat over the other two sets of points. Pin the cut ends to the star. Pin the braid here and there with small pins, each threaded through a pearl bead.

3 Thread a hat pin through the filigree cone. Dip the part of the pin showing below the cone in tacky glue; place it on one of the star points. Repeat with the other five points.

4 Push a hat pin through the polystyrene on each side of the filigree cone. Angle them so that they do not poke through the other side.

5 Push a hat pin in each space at the centre of the star where the braid strips cross over (six in all). Repeat on the other side.

6 Thread the small pearls onto a small pin. Poke these into the star in a line all around

the outside edge between the filigree cones. Place a second row just inside the first row on each side. Place two rows of pearls from the centre of the star, halfway between the braid strips in the six sections of the star, to the outside edge, which is decorated with two rows of pearls. Repeat on the back. The star will now have six diamond-shaped sections outlined with two rows of pearl beads, with gold cord running through the centre of the diamond shape and a filigree cone on the outside strip.

White and gold tree-top star

7 Place small pearls threaded onto a short pin randomly in the gold sections on each side of the gold braid. Repeat on the back.

8 Poke a hole on each side of the centre of the star at the back. Glue a 4in (10cm) length of wire in each side. Use this for attaching the star to the top of the tree.

SEQUINNED MINI-BELL

MATERIALS

Polystyrene mini-bell shape

Pencil

20in (50cm) red or white ribbon with gold metallic
diamonds, ⅜in (9mm) wide

200 brass pins, 14 x .55mm

200 gold or red cup sequins, ¼in (6mm)

150 tiny crystal glass beads

1⅔yd (1.5m) gold metallic ribbon, ¼in (6mm) wide

2 white or gold teardrop hat pins or corsage pins,
2in (5cm) long

2 medium crystal or gold cut plastic beads

1 small flat filigree gold cap

1 Divide each polystyrene shape into four
equal sections using a pencil. Sections should
run up and down the length of the shape.

2 Cover the pencil lines using the ribbon
with the metallic diamond design. Instead of
starting at the top of the mini-bell, start by
placing the first cut end of the ribbon into the
hole at the bottom or wide end, run the ribbon around the shape and back to the hole,
pushing the second cut end into the hole too.
Use short pins to hold the ribbon in place on
the edge of the hole. Repeat with a second
piece of ribbon at right angles to the first.

3 Fill in the sections between the ribbon
with 'cup up' bead and sequin units, using
gold or red sequins and tiny clear beads. Work
in rows from the outside towards the centre.

4 Make a double set of ribbon loops over
two opposite sequinned sections, using gold
metallic ribbon.

Sequinned mini-bells

5 Make a hanging loop with gold metallic ribbon. Position it to run right and left over the ribbon loops placed so that when the ornament is held up by the hanger, the ribbon loops are on each side of the mini-bell.

6 To decorate and complete the ornament, make two of the following units and place one each into the centre top (over the ribbon loops) and centre bottom (over hole) of the mini-bell. Onto a teardrop hat pin (white for the white/gold bell; red for the red/gold bell) thread on one medium cut plastic bead (crystal for white/gold; gold for red/gold) and a flat filigree cap (convex).

SEQUINNED FILIGREE OVAL

MATERIALS

2in (5cm) oval (or spherical) moulded polystyrene shape
40in (1m) gold metallic grosgrain ribbon, ⅛in (3mm) wide
400 brass pins, 14 x .55mm
350 tiny clear or red glass beads
350 mother-of-pearl or red cup sequins, ¼in (6mm)
40in (1m) gold metallic grosgrain ribbon, ⅜in (9mm) wide
1 gold filigree cone
2 white or gold teardrop hat pins, 2in (5cm) long
12 long dressmaking pins
6 small amber or red cut glass beads
6 medium white pearl or gold oat beads
6 small white pearl or gold oat beads
6 white or gold pearl beads, ⅛in (3mm)
1 gold rhinestone bead
1 plastic gold cap

1 Divide each polystyrene shape into six equal sections using a pencil. Ensure that the sections run along the length of the shape (up and down).

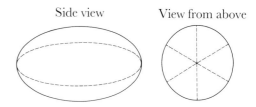

Side view   View from above

2 Cover the pencil lines with the narrower gold ribbon, and secure with brass pins.

3 Fill in the blank sections with 'cup up' bead and sequin units using clear beads and mother-of-pearl sequins for the white/gold ornament or red beads and red sequins for the red/gold ornament.

4 Place one set of double loops across two opposite sequinned sections using the wider ribbon.

5 Make a hanging loop using narrower ribbon. Position hanging loop to run right and left over ribbon loops placed so that when the ornament is held up by the hanging loop, the ribbon loops are on each side of the oval shape.

6 Bend the six prongs of the filigree cone so that they hug the oval shape when placed at the bottom of the ornament. Pass a hat pin through from the tip to attach the cone to the bottom of the decoration. Position the prongs to extend into the sequinned sections, removing any sequin units if necessary.

7 Make up six units of a long pin passed through a cut glass bead and a medium pearl oat bead (white pearl for the white/gold ornament; gold for the red/gold ornament). Place one of these units at the point between each of the prongs of the filigree cone.

8 Make up six units of a long pin passed through a small pearl oat bead (white pearl for white/gold; gold for the red/gold ornament). Place one of these units in front of each of the large oat units.

Sequinned filigree ornaments and round sequin decorations

9 Make up six units of a long pin passed through a small pearl bead (white pearl for white/gold; gold for the red/gold). Place two of these in the three prongs with cut-outs.

10 To complete the sequinned filigree ornament, place one final unit of a hat pin (white for the white/gold; gold for the red/gold) passed through a gold rhinestone bead and a gold plastic cap (convex) in the centre of the top of the decoration, over the top of the ribbon loops.

ROUND SEQUIN DECORATION

MATERIALS

Round (or oval) moulded polystyrene shape,
2in (5cm) in diameter

Pencil

20in (50cm) gold-edged (white or red) satin ribbon,
³⁄₈in (9mm) wide

20in (50cm) gold-edged (white or red) satin ribbon,
¹⁄₈in (3mm) wide

1²⁄₃–2¹⁄₄yd (1.5–2m) gold metallic ribbon,
¹⁄₄in (6mm) wide

200 white or gold pearls, ¹⁄₈in (3mm)

500 brass pins, 14 x .55mm

125 mother-of-pearl or red cup sequins, ¹⁄₄in (6mm)

125 tiny clear or red glass beads

150 matt gold cup sequins, ¹⁄₄in (6mm)

2 white or gold teardrop hat pins, 2in (5cm) long

3 tiny gold beads

1 small crystal or red cut glass bead

2 gold filigree caps

1 medium crystal or red cut glass bead

1 large crystal or red cut glass bead

1 Divide each polystyrene shape into four equal sections using a pencil. Sections should run up and down the length of the shape.

2 Cover the pencil lines with the wider gold-edged satin ribbon (white satin ribbon for the white/gold ornament and red satin ribbon for the red/gold ornament). Repeat the process with the narrower gold-edged satin ribbon, running it down the middle of the wider ribbon. This creates a strip of ribbon with four gold stripes.

3 Place a row of pearl units (a small pearl bead threaded onto a short pin) into the polystyrene shape along the edges of the ribbon in each of the four blank sections between the ribbon (white pearls for the white/gold ornament; gold pearls for the red/gold ornament).

4 Along the edge of the pearl units, place a row of 'cup down' matt gold sequin units.

5 Fill in the remaining blank space with rows of 'cup-up' bead and sequin units (clear glass beads and mother-of-pearl sequins for the white/gold ball and red beads and sequins for the red/gold ball).

6 Make a double set of loops over two opposite sequinned sections using the gold metallic ribbon.

7 Using the same gold metallic ribbon, make a second set of double loops over the remaining two opposite sequinned sections, at right angles to the first.

8 Form a hanging loop and place it on the top of the ornament across the ribbon loops.

9 Decorate and complete the ornament by placing the hat pin units listed below in the centre top (over the ribbon loops) and the centre bottom.

TOP UNIT

This consists of a teardrop hat pin (white for the white/gold ornament, red for the red/gold ornament) passed through a tiny gold bead, a small crystal cut glass bead and a gold filigree cap (convex).

BOTTOM UNIT

This comprises a teardrop hat pin (white for white/gold; red for red/gold) passed through a tiny gold bead, a medium crystal cut glass bead, a tiny gold bead, a large crystal cut glass bead and a gold filigree cap (concave).

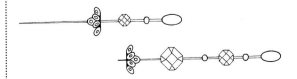

ACCORDIAN ANGELS

MATERIALS

12in (30cm) paper ribbon, approximately
3½in (9cm) wide

Scissors

Rub-on face

Tape measure

4in (10cm) gold chenille glitter stem (or a 12in (30cm)
pipe cleaner cut into thirds)

18in (45cm) wire

1 head bead, ¾in (2cm)

Doll hair

1 bow, ½–¾in (12mm–2cm)

Tacky glue

1 Cut the ribbon into three pieces: one piece measuring 8in (20cm) for the dress (body), and two pieces each 2in (5cm) for the sleeves.

2 Pleat the three pieces of ribbon concertina fashion along their width. Make the pleats ¼in (6mm) wide and 3½in (9cm) long.

3 Place the glitter stem between folds at centre back of the longer piece of ribbon. Pinch up one end of ribbon around the glitter stem. Wind one end of wire twice around the ribbon and glitter stem, about ¼in (6mm) from end of the ribbon.

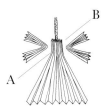

4 Take one of the smaller pieces of pleated ribbon (see diagram). Fold in half and butt the fold to point 'A'. Use the same wire to bind this sleeve to the glitter stem, through centre fold of sleeve. Repeat with the other sleeve at point 'B'. Pull wire around and twist at the back. Use it to attach the angel to the tree.

5 Thread a head bead onto the glitter stem protruding above the dress and sleeves. Push it down until it touches the top edge of ribbon. Use the excess glitter stem to form a halo by twisting it around your finger, above the head bead. Glue hair onto the head bead, and rub the face onto the bead, following the manufacturer's instructions.

6 Glue a tiny bow over the wire at the front of the angel's dress.

FLUFFY DOUBLE-LOOP BOW

MATERIALS

Scissors

54in (135cm) matt gold paper ribbon twist,
approximately 2in (5cm) wide

36in (90cm) florist's wire

Gold acrylic paint

Paintbrush or sponge

1 Cut two strips of ribbon 8in (20cm) long, and two strips of ribbon 12in (30cm) long, leaving one strip of ribbon 14in (35cm) long.

2 Fold one 8in (20cm) strip of ribbon in half. Scrunch it up along this central line and hold; then form loops with each of the cut ends of the paper strips by overlapping ¼–½in (6–12mm). Wrap the bow with wire. Repeat with the other 8in (20cm) ribbon strip.

3 Place the two sets of loops formed with the 8in (20cm) strips of ribbon side by side. Wire them together, side by side.

4 Repeat steps 2 and 3 with the 12in (30cm) strips of ribbon.

5 Place the small set of ribbon loops over the larger set of ribbon loops. Take the 14in

(35cm) ribbon strip, scrunch the centre and place it over the middle of the two sets of bow loops. Wrap this strip of ribbon around to the back of the bow loops and tie the ends in a single knot, pulling tightly to hold (you could wire the two sets of ribbon loops together first if desired).

6 Pull the bow tails down and cut V-notches in the tail ends. Fluff out the bow loops.

Accordian angel

7 Paint the bow very lightly with gold acrylic paint using a paintbrush or sponge.

8 Thread a 6in (15cm) piece of wire through the back of the bow. Use this to attach the bow to the tree, wreath, swag, serviette or wrapped parcel.

MINIATURE PARCELS AND CRACKERS

On pages 97 and 99 you will find the instructions for making these small gift ornaments and miniature crackers. For my colour themes I have used a gold foil wrapping paper which has been decorated with ribbon curls made from florist's ribbon. The curls have then been shredded with a ribbon shredder to make the curls much finer, giving a more delicate appearance.

CLOTHBALLS

MATERIALS

Moulded polystyrene shapes
Pencil
Tape measure
Tissue paper
Scissors
Christmas fabric, 6 x 3in (15 x 7.5cm)
Tacky glue
40–80in (1–2m) ribbon
12in (30cm) lace or braid
Short pins
Long dressmaking pins
Hat pins, cut crystal beads and filigree caps

1 Make a paper pattern by dividing the polystyrene shape into four equal sections. Mark the sections with a pencil and measure them to ensure they are equal. Lay a piece of tissue paper over one section and trace out the pattern from the lines on the polystyrene. Cut out the pattern and check that it fits. Although this pattern can now be used over and over again when covering that particular shape and size of polystyrene, it is advisable to section off each shape lightly with a pencil before moving on to the next step.

2 Using the pattern made, cut out four pieces of fabric for each ornament.

3 Spread a thin line of tacky glue along the inside of the pencil lines all the way around one section. Place a piece of fabric over the glue. Press down the two points of fabric and then run a finger down the centre of the fabric, smoothing it out over the curve of the shape. Ease in the edges of the fabric to prevent tucks appearing. Very tiny tucks along the edge will not show after they have been covered with lace, ribbon or braid. Glue fabric pieces to the remaining three sections on the polystyrene shape. As you are working, trim away any fabric that overlaps onto another section. Do not worry about very small gaps between fabric pieces as these can be covered by ribbon, lace or braid.

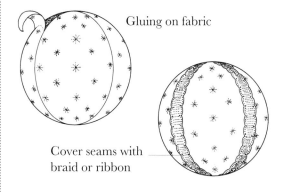

Gluing on fabric

Cover seams with braid or ribbon

4 Cover the seams between fabric pieces using lace, ribbon or braid. Pin them in place at the top and bottom of the shape.

5 There are many ways to decorate the top of this ornament using ribbons. You can form ribbon loops, as given in steps 5–7, or see alternatives in step 8. To make the ribbon loops, take two long pins and place them so that they are firmly fixed, yet protruding, about one-third of the way down from the top

Opposite *Miniature parcels, crackers and clothballs*

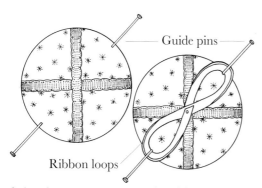

Guide pins

Ribbon loops

of the shape on two opposite sides in the centre of the section. These will act as guide pins and should be removed after the ribbon loops are completed. Fix one cut end of the ribbon to the centre top of the shape. Keep the ribbon flat (do not twist it) and wind it clockwise around one guide pin, then back to the beginning. Continue winding the ribbon, this time anti-clockwise, around the other guide pin. Check to see that this figure-of-eight set of loops is of equal length and fullness on both sides. Fix in place with short pins.

6 Make a second set of loops directly over the previous set, but do *not* cut the ribbon. Replace the guide pins ¼in (6mm) closer to the top of the shape. Use the same technique to form another set of loops directly over the first ones, but a little smaller. This can be repeated for a third set of loops, and so on.

7 To form a set of loops at right angles to the first set of loops, first cut the ribbon. Start again, this time forming the loops described in step 5 over the other two sections.

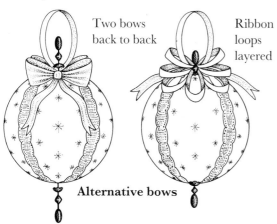

Two bows back to back

Ribbon loops layered

Alternative bows

8 Alternatively, you can tie two simple bows and place them back to back with the hanging loop from step 9 placed between them. Or you could stack several layers of bow loops to form a pompom bow with the hanging loop extending from the top of the bow.

9 To form a hanging loop, take 6–8in (15–20cm) of ribbon and form a large loop, overlapping the two cut ends. Fix these cut ends centrally on the top of the ornament between the ribbon loops, using short pins.

10 Now decorate the top and bottom of the ornament with a hat pin passed through a cut crystal bead and a filigree cap or your choice of jewellery findings. These will cover any pins or cut ends of ribbons.

GEMSTONE ORNAMENTS

MATERIALS

Papier mâché ornaments (stars, hearts, bells, etc)
Gold acrylic paint
Paintbrush
Tacky glue
Flat-backed artificial gemstones
Gold cord and braids

1 Paint the papier mâché shapes with two or more coats of gold acrylic paint, allowing the paint to dry thoroughly between coats.

2 Decorate the papier mâché shapes by gluing on gemstones, cord and braid. For example, you could use the cord or braid to divide the ornament into sections, which you can then decorate with gemstones. Use your imaginative skills to make creative designs.

Opposite *Gemstone ornaments*

Table Setting

Gold reflects a lavish brilliance and richness in both the red and white table settings. Elegant beaded linen, using a simple but classic poinsettia design, forms the background to the splendid golden centrepiece. The stylish Italian bonbonniere filled with enticing handmade chocolates makes an exquisite focus to a very sophisticated dinner table.

Gold and white table setting

BEADED TABLE LINEN

BASIC BEADING TECHNIQUES

This is a special technique for using fabric paint to make paint dots that resemble beads. It is important to use a fabric paint that has the appropriate consistency for making self-rounding beads. It should be machine-washable, it should not require heat setting and it usually comes in a bottle with the appropriate tip for forming beads (see page 127 for list of craft suppliers).

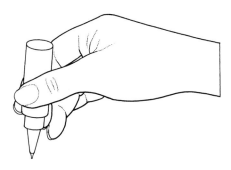

To get the paint into the tip of the bottle, shake the bottle two or three times with a hard, fast motion. You will feel the paint drop forwards. Hold the bottle close to the surface of the fabric in an almost vertical position.

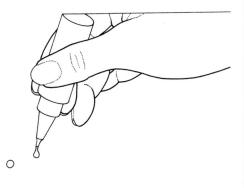

Squeeze the bottle slowly and, as the paint touches the surface and expands towards the bottle tip, lift it slightly while continuing to

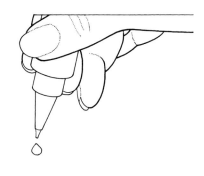

squeeze out paint until you achieve the bead size you require. Stop squeezing and lift the tip away from the bead. The paint should never envelope the bottle tip.

After every fourth or fifth bead, wipe the tip of the bottle on a piece of kitchen paper. Continue to shake the paint down into the bottle tip at regular intervals. Allow the beading to dry for 72 hours before using the fabric.

Before you begin, it is advisable to practise on a piece of scrap fabric or paper first to help you get used to the beading technique.

Do not machine-wash or dry-clean beaded fabric. Hand wash only in mild detergent and at a cool temperature. Do not soak, wring, stretch or twist the fabric as this could damage the 'beads'. Hang or lay the fabric flat to dry. The cloth may be ironed by covering the board surface with a soft towel and placing the beads down into towel. Press lightly on wrong side with a steam iron. Allow to cool before removing.

MATERIALS
Pre-made tablecloth and serviettes
Tracing paper
Pencil
Long dressmaking pins
Cardboard
Straight pins
Dimensional fabric paint with beading consistency
Kitchen paper

1 Wash a pre-made tablecloth and serviettes without conditioner to remove sizing. Dry and then press the fabric to remove all creases.

2 To transfer the poinsettia pattern on page 125 to the tablecloth or serviettes, place a piece of tracing paper over the pattern. With a pencil, trace the dots onto the paper. Poke holes through the dots of the pattern with a dressmaking pin. Position the paper pattern on the tablecloth or serviettes. Use the pencil to mark the dots through the hole, onto the tablecloth or serviettes. Repeat the design as desired around the edge of the tablecloth. It is not recommended to bead the top of the tablecloth where plates and serving dishes could tip over because of the uneven surface the beads would create.

3 Place a large piece of clean, dry cardboard (the side of a cardboard box will work fine) flat on the work surface. Place a section of the fabric to be beaded over the cardboard. Hold it taut with dressmaking pins poked through the fabric to the cardboard around the design.

4 Working from the top left towards the bottom right (top right to bottom left if left-handed), bead the design. Work with one colour at a time, allowing the beads to dry for at least 12–24 hours before continuing with the next colour. Wipe the bottle on a piece of kitchen paper after every fourth or fifth bead.

5 Outline the beads with a continuous line of dimensional fabric paint.

CHRISTMAS BONBONNIERE

MATERIALS

3 tulle nets

1 plastic cup

Handmade chocolates, mints, etc

18in (45cm) ribbon

Decorations

1 Lay the tulle nets directly on top of each other on a flat surface. Place the plastic cup with your choice of chocolates, sweets or mints in the centre of the three nets.

2 Draw together the layers around the plastic cup and hold them firmly in one hand.

3 Tie the ribbon around the bonbonnière, making two even loops. Tie a bow to secure.

4 Pull the outer net downwards against the ribbon, working all the way around until it has separated from the other layers. Continue with each net, working inwards until the layers are separated and fluffy. Pull the final layer quite firmly so that you can just see the chocolates or mints inside.

5 Decorate the bonbonnière with a selection of your favourite embellishments.

Christmas bonbonnière

GOLDEN CENTREPIECE

MATERIALS

6in (15cm) ceramic urn, 6in (15cm) in diameter

Gold aerosol paint

2 artichokes

9in (22.5cm) gold pillar candle, 3in (7.5cm) in diameter

3 bunches of artificial damsons

7 bunches of dried leaves

15 saligmum stems (or similar dried pods, cones, etc)

Handful of string moss

3 twig branches, approximately 10in (25cm) long

Ribbon

Stiff florist's wire

Hard, dry florist's compound

1 Hang the artichokes upside down and leave to dry thoroughly. This can take as long as three or four weeks, depending on the humidity and temperature.

2 Spray the urn, dried artichokes, damsons, leaves, saligmum, string moss and twigs with gold aerosol paint. Work in a well-ventilated area and allow the paint to dry before proceeding. Sometimes a second coat will be required. Several light mistings are preferable to one very thick coat of paint, which could drip as well as take much longer to dry.

3 Wire the artichokes by wrapping the stem with wire leaving two tails to extend 3–4in (7.5–10cm) below the end of the stem. This will be used to secure the artichokes in the florist's compound.

4 Wire together the leaves in bunches with wire extending below the stem to secure into the arrangement.

Red and gold table setting

5 Place the candle in the centre of the urn. Pack dry florist's compound around the candle and up to the rim of the urn to secure it.

6 Place the artichokes on each side of the candle, towards the front of the urn.

7 Place one bunch of damsons at the front of the candle, between the two artichokes.

A Christmas wreath

Place the other two bunches behind the candle, spaced an equal distance apart.

8 Place one twig branch in the front of the arrangement, between the damsons and the candle. Place the other two branches towards

the back of the arrangement, behind the artichokes.

9 Make a simple looped bow using a 30in (75cm) piece of wired ribbon. Fold it in half to find the centre and scrunch this together along the width of the ribbon, point A.

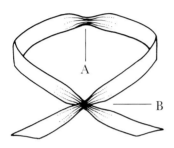

Measure 8in (20cm) from each end, overlap and scrunch along the width of the ribbon, point B. Bring together points A and B and wrap firmly with stiff florist's wire. Twist the ends of the wire together to form a tail to poke into the arrangement.

10 Place the simple looped bow in the gap between the damsons and the twig branch at the front of the arrangement.

11 Fill in the gaps and spaces around the arrangement with saligmum and bunches of leaves. Fill any gaps close to the edge of the urn with string moss.

A Christmas Wreath

This Christmas wreath makes a simple but elegant decoration for any door. I have chosen a thick golden cord which is twisted among the lush fir branches. Striking bows with furled tails form the focal point, and these are accented by miniature parcels and crackers.

MATERIALS

Pre-made fir wreath
2yd (1.8m) gold cord
Florist's wire
4 Fluffy Double-loop Bows (see page 10)
2 Miniature Crackers (see page 99)
2 Parcel Ornaments (see page 97)

1 Starting from the back of the wreath, weave gold cord in and out of the branches, all around the wreath. Secure the ends in place with small pieces of florist's wire. To secure the cord further, attach it to the fir branches at regular intervals with wire.

2 Attach the four fluffy double-loop bows to the wreath with florist's wire, spacing them evenly around the wreath. Ensure that the florist's wire is concealed behind the branches of the wreath.

3 Decorate the remaining gaps on the wreath with a few of the same miniature crackers and parcel ornaments as were used on the Christmas tree, wiring them neatly in position. Use any variety and number of decorations you desire: be as creative as your time and imagination allow.

CHAPTER 3

A Tartan Theme

*I*N RECENT YEARS the use of various Scottish tartans has become more popular in interior home decor. The combination of rich red, deep green and burnished gold in the form of a bold plaid pattern lends itself perfectly to a cosy Christmas theme.

The same tartan fabric in the form of lovely bows is used repeatedly to provide fresh and luxuriant colour not only on this Yuletide tree but throughout the chapter's decorations. Perfectly shaped bows with ruched tails can be found on the welcoming wreath at the front door, within the fir branches of the fireplace swag, adorning the wine basket and mounted on the back of the Golden Swan Centrepiece (see page 54).

The tartan theme lends itself perfectly as a backdrop to many other themes. You could add a collection of ornaments to reflect a special personal or family preference, or include artificial apples, oranges and plums for a fruity look. Regardless of your heritage, the Scottish tartan makes an attractive theme.

Tree Decorations

For this tartan theme I have chosen a mixture of natural textures and brilliant metals which are woven together by a profusion of lush tartan fabric. The Christmas evergreen reflects this blend of rugged simplicity in nature as depicted by the Pine Cone Angel and Bird in a Nest ornaments (see page 42). Bundles of heather tied together with satin ribbons, along with dried thistles, lend authenticity, while miniature boxes and crackers add lightness to the earthy sombreness.

STIFFENED TREE BOWS

MATERIALS

Scissors

1yd (90cm) Christmas tartan fabric, 45in (1.1m) wide
(makes about 18 bows)

Aluminium foil

Sticky tape

Fabric stiffener

Coat hangers and pegs

Iron

90-gauge wire

Low temperature glue gun and glue sticks

Soft plastic wrap, for stuffing

Water-based glaze

Paintbrush

1 For each tree bow cut the following fabric strips: 1 streamer piece – 3 x 13in (7.5 x 32.5cm); 1 bow loop piece – 3 x 14in (7.5 x 35cm); and 1 connector piece – ½ x 4in (12mm x 10cm).

2 Lay the aluminium foil down flat on your work surface. Secure it in place with sticky tape around the edges if possible, ensuring that it is taut. Place the streamer piece on top of the foil with the right side of the fabric facing upwards.

3 Pour a small amount of fabric stiffener down the centre of the fabric. Spread it over the entire piece with your fingers. Turn the fabric over and repeat on the wrong side. Repeat this process with the bow loop piece and the connector piece for all the bows.

4 Hang all the pieces of fabric by a short end (not in the middle) on coat hangers using pegs. Let them dry thoroughly.

5 When completely dry, remove the pieces from the hanger and run a medium hot iron over both sides of one set of pieces – streamer, bow loops and connector. Work with just one set of strips at a time. The heat will make the stiffened fabric more flexible. Bows should be formed while the pieces are soft.

6 To form the bow, fold the streamer piece in half along its length to determine the centre. Form two or three small pleats across the width at the centre; hold in place with a peg.

7 Place the bow loop piece onto the work surface with the wrong side of the fabric facing upwards. Find the centre and bring the ends of the strip together, overlapping the centre and each other by at least ½in (12mm). Gather the folded strip in the centre with

three pleats, as with the streamer piece. Hold in place with a peg.

8 To assemble, place the bow loops over the streamer, matching pleated centres. Place an 8in (20cm) wire (90 gauge) along the back side of the streamer. The wire is used to attach bows to the tree. Tightly wrap the connector strip twice around the bow loops, streamer and wire. Glue in place with low temperature hot glue.

9 Stuff each of the bow loops carefully with balls of plastic wrap to shape them. Trim the streamers to the desired length with a V-shaped notch.

10 Paint the bow with two thin layers of water-based glaze to seal and protect it. When dry, remove the balls of plastic wrap and paint the inside of the loops with a layer of water-based glaze.

Stiffened tree bow and miniature tree crackers (see page 42)

MINIATURE PARCELS AND CRACKERS

For the parcels, follow the instructions given on page 97 for making parcel ornaments. For this Tartan theme I have used matt paper in red or green and decorated the parcels with raffia tied into small bows.

For the crackers, follow the instructions given on page 99. I made several crackers using recycled paper in two different colours – a rustic red and a sombre green to echo the more masculine mood of the tartan tree. To add extra brightness, you could use plaid foil in the same colours as the tartan fabric tree bows. The crackers were then decorated with raffia tied around each end.

PINE CONE ANGEL

MATERIALS

Low temperature glue gun and glue sticks
1 medium-sized acorn with cap
1 pine cone, 4-6in (10-15cm long)
3-4in (7.5-10cm) natural brown paper wire
1 small sprig green moss
1 piece dried brown leaf
6in (15cm) dark green satin ribbon, $^1/_{16}$ in (1.5mm) wide
Small white cedar cones
2 dried milkweed pods
3in (7.5cm) fine wire

1 Glue the acorn to the top of the pine cone with the bottom facing towards the front, pointing down slightly.

2 Fold the cut ends of the paper wire back. Tuck the centre of the wire in between the petals on the cone, about 1in (2.5cm) above the stem. Bend the open ends of the wire towards the centre front, to form hands.

3 Glue the moss in between the hands, then glue a dried leaf over the moss.

4 Cut the ribbon in half and form two loops. Overlap them and glue them over the leaf. Glue on the white cedar cones.

5 Glue the two milkweed pods to the centre of the back of the cone to form wings. Glue a small wire loop at the back for the hanger.

BIRD IN A NEST

MATERIALS

Scissors
Tape measure
1yd (90cm) red satin ribbon, $^1/_4$ in (6mm) wide
Low temperature glue gun and glue sticks
1 small nest-shaped basket, 2-3in (5-7.5cm) in diameter
Cloth-covered wire
Red raffia
2 stems of green moss
1 small artificial (mushroom) bird
Gypsophila

1 Cut two 7in (17.5cm) pieces of ribbon. Turn all cut ends under and glue the ends of the ribbons to the sides of the basket so that they criss-cross over the basket.

2 Gather the ribbon tightly with wire at the top where the ribbons cross over. With the remaining ribbon, form a double-loop bow and glue this to the wired ribbon.

3 Fill the nest with raffia. Glue green moss to the nest in one section between the two ribbons. Add the bird and attach a small piece of raffia to the bird's beak. Glue gypsophila to the moss to add little highlights.

Opposite *Angel, bird in a nest and miniature parcel*

Room Decorations

To extend the tartan theme throughout your home, why not make some of the exciting projects in this section. Hang a Christmas swag decorated with pine cones, ornaments and tartan bows over your mantelpiece, or enliven your dining room with a wine basket painted green and decorated with a festive tartan bow. Traditionalists might prefer to make a Christmas stocking and decorate it with one of the colourful ideas in this section. Alternatively, you can make a wreath arrangement from fir, holly, tartan bows and a resplendent french horn to complete the tartan look.

FRENCH HORN SWAG

MATERIALS

Pre-made swag (see pages 106-107)

Florist's wire

6 Stiffened Tree Bows (see page 40)

Low temperature glue gun and glue sticks (optional)

Assorted pine cones

French horn wreath (see page 49)

8 Pine Cone Angel ornaments (see page 42)

8 Miniature Parcels (see page 42)

8 Miniature Crackers (see page 42)

1 Hang the pre-made swag in position on the mantelpiece in your preferred style. Referring to the photograph above for guidance, wire a stiffened tree bow into each of the outer corners of the swag. Take care to conceal the wire in the branches of the swag. Wire or glue pine cones of various shapes and sizes to form a cluster above each bow.

2 Wire the French horn wreath in the middle of the swag (if a nail or hook is holding up the swag, hang and wire the French horn to this). Attach one stiffened tree bow to the swag halfway between the centrepiece and the outside corner. Attach another bow halfway down the tail of the swag. Repeat on the other side of the swag.

French horn swag and wine basket (see page 46)

3 Wire the pine cone angels, and miniature parcels and crackers in between the bows.

4 Attach as many other pine cones, bows and ornaments as space allows.

WINE BASKET

MATERIALS

Divided wine basket
Christmas green aerosol paint
Paintbrush
Gold acrylic paint
Scissors
½yd (50cm) Christmas tartan fabric, 36 or 45in
(90cm or 1.1m) wide
Tape measure
Aluminium foil
Sticky tape
Fabric stiffener
Coat hanger and pegs
Low temperature glue gun and glue sticks
Soft plastic wrap, for stuffing
Water-based glaze

1 In a well-ventilated area, spray the basket with several light mistings of green aerosol paint. Allow the paint to dry thoroughly between coats.

2 Using a paintbrush, paint the rim of the basket with two coats of gold acrylic paint, allowing the first coat to dry before applying the second.

3 Cut the fabric into three strips, in the following sizes:
1 streamer piece – 8 x 30in (20 x 75cm);
1 bow loop piece – 8 x 18in (20 x 45cm);
1 connector piece – 4 x 10in (10 x 25cm).

4 Follow the simple instructions given for making a stiffened bow as in steps 2-14 on pages 49-50.

5 Glue the bow into position at the front of the basket, or wherever desired.

Opposite *Christmas stockings*

CHRISTMAS STOCKINGS

MATERIALS

Felt in co-ordinating colour, 24 x 16in (60 x 40cm)
Scissors
Tartan fabric, 1yd x 14in (90 x 35cm)
Tape measure
Fusible adhesive
Iron
Needle and cotton
Ribbon for hanger

MAKING THE STOCKINGS

1 Enlarge the pattern on pages 122–123 by 150 per cent. Fold the felt in half to form a piece measuring 12 x 16in (30 x 40cm). Cut two enlarged, full stocking patterns from the felt. One piece will form the front and one piece will form the back of the stocking. From the tartan fabric cut one piece measuring 14½ x 10in (36.5 x 25cm) for the contrasting stocking top and two pieces each of the contrasting toe and heel pieces. From the fusible adhesive, cut two pieces each of the toe and heel pieces, about ⅛in (3mm) smaller than the enlarged pattern.

2 Using an iron on a warm setting, apply the fusible adhesive to the wrong side of the tartan toe and heel fabric pieces, following the manufacturer's instructions. Then apply the tartan heel and toe pieces to the right sides of the felt stocking pieces, both on the front and the back.

3 Decorate the front stocking piece as desired (see ideas on page 48).

4 Place the two felt stocking pieces together, with wrong sides facing. Stitch around the outside of the pieces, ⅛in (3mm) from the cut edge, leaving the top open.

5 Fold the tartan fabric in half so that the two short ends are together and the right sides are facing. Hand-stitch or machine the short ends together allowing a $\frac{1}{4}$ in (6mm) seam. This forms the contrasting cuff for the top of the stocking.

6 Place the cuff outside the top edge of the stocking with right sides together. Stitch around the top edge leaving a $\frac{1}{4}$ in (6mm) seam allowance. Pull the cuff above the stocking top and fold it down halfway. Turn under the raw edge of the cuff about 1in (12mm) and hand-stitch to the inside of the felt stocking, using a blind stitch.

7 Hand-stitch a loop of ribbon in either a matching or contrasting colour in the top corner of the stocking, on the same side as the heel. This will form the hanger.

DECORATING THE STOCKINGS

APPLIQUÉD CHRISTMAS TREE

MATERIALS
Green, brown, red, white and blue felt
2oz (60g) wadding
Tartan fabric, 2 x 10in (5 x 25cm)
Ribbon
White pearl beads
Gold charms

1 Using the tree template on page 124, cut out a tree shape from the green felt and the wadding. Trim the wadding tree piece down by about $\frac{1}{8}$ in (3mm) all the way around. Cut out one piece of brown felt, measuring 2in x $1\frac{1}{2}$ in (5 x 4cm), for the tree trunk. Cut out two pieces each of various colours and sizes of felt to make parcels.

2 Place the green felt tree over the tree-shaped wadding piece and place into position on the front felt stocking piece. Starting from the top, hand-stitch around the tree. Roll up the piece of brown felt for the trunk and stitch it to the bottom of the tree.

3 Sew a $\frac{1}{4}$ in (6mm) hem along one long edge of the tartan fabric. Gather the opposite long end to form a ruffle. Stitch the gathered end around the tree trunk, forming a tree skirt. Allow the ruffle to hang free.

4 To make the parcels, place a small amount of wadding between the two pieces of felt. Hand-stitch around the edges. Stitch or glue ribbon around the seam to hide the stitches. Add a strip of ribbon around the front side and ribbon loops to the top.

5 Hand-stitch tiny white pearl beads on the tree, looping them from side to side to form the garland. Stitch on small gold charms for tree ornaments.

APPLIQUÉD POINSETTIA

MATERIALS
Fusible adhesive
Poinsettia-patterned fabric
Dimensional fabric paints

1 Following the manufacturer's instructions, iron the fusible adhesive to the wrong side of the poinsettia-patterned fabric. Cut out the flowers and leaves required and position these on the front felt stocking piece.

2 Following the manufacturer's instructions, remove the backing paper and fuse the poinsettia into position using a warm iron.

3 Using dimensional fabric paints, apply a bead of paint around the poinsettia petals and leaves to highlight the design. To do this, squeeze the bottle of paint carefully to produce an even line.

FRENCH HORN WREATH

MATERIALS

Scissors

½yd (50cm) Christmas tartan fabric, 36 or 45in (90cm or 1.1m) wide

Tape measure

Aluminium foil

Sticky tape

Fabric stiffener

Coat hanger and pegs

Large French horn, 12in (30cm) in diameter

Low temperature glue gun and glue sticks

Soft plastic wrap, for stuffing

Water-based glaze

Paintbrush

Green florist's wire

Small pieces of fir

Holly and berries

Sprigs of heather

Fir cones

Sprigs of gypsophila

MAKING A STIFFENED BOW

1 Cut the fabric into three strips, in the following sizes:
1 streamer piece – 8 x 30in (20 x 75cm);
1 bow loop piece – 8 x 18in (20 x 45cm);
1 connector piece – 3 x 10in (7.5 x 25cm).

2 Lay a piece of aluminium foil down on the work surface. The aluminium foil should be a little longer than the longest fabric strip; for the large single-looped bow, that would be 32in (80cm) long. Secure with tape.

3 Place the long streamer piece on the aluminium foil with the right side of the fabric facing. Pour fabric stiffener down the centre of the fabric strip and spread it evenly all over the piece with your hands. Turn the strip over and repeat on the wrong side of the fabric.

4 Place the bow loop piece directly over the streamer piece with the wrong side of the fabric facing upwards. Smooth the fabric over the streamer piece to absorb any excess stiffener. Add more fabric stiffener and spread it over the strip with your hands until it is thoroughly covered.

5 Place the connector piece directly over the bow loop piece, with the wrong side facing upwards, and coat it with the fabric stiffener as before.

6 Fold the connector piece into thirds along the length. Start with one long edge and fold over 1in (2.5cm). Fold over the other long edge to form a strip 10in (25cm) long and 1in (2.5cm) wide. Put this on one side while folding the remaining strips of fabric.

7 Fold one long edge of the bow loop piece to the centre, overlapping it by about ¼in (6mm). Fold the other long edge to the centre of the strip and overlap slightly to form a strip of fabric 25in (62.5cm) long and just under 8in (20cm) wide. Using your hands, press a deep crease in the folds. This makes crisp, flat edges and removes wrinkles, air bubbles and any excess fabric stiffener. Put this piece on one side and use the same technique to fold the streamer piece.

8 Gently lift the fabric strips one at a time and hang on a clothes line or coat hanger to dry. Hang each strip from the end (not the middle) and secure with a peg. Check that the back seam of the bow loop piece is held together so that the piece will dry flat.

9 Let the strips dry until they are crisp on the outside but still damp on the inside. At normal room temperature this takes about 30 to 40 minutes. The fabric strip should be dry enough to hold the shape of the bow but with some flexibility to allow the bow to be formed.

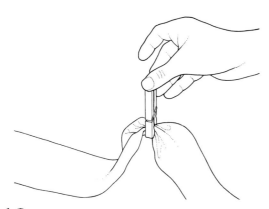

10 Gently fold the streamer piece in half across the width to give you two bow tails of equal length (15in (38cm) each). Gather the fabric along the width of the strip, squeezing the fabric from one side to the other to form about three gathers or pleats. Hold these pleats in place with a large peg and set aside until ready to assemble the bow.

11 Place the bow loop piece on the work surface with the seam side facing upwards. Trim off any threads from frayed edges. Mark the centre of the strip. Bring the ends of the bow loop piece to the centre and overlap them by 1in (2.5cm). Gather the fabric tightly along the centre, forming about three pleats where the ends have overlapped. Hold in place with another peg. Check that the bow loops are of equal size and fullness.

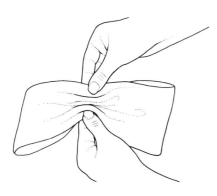

12 For the French horn wreath, go straight to steps 15–19. To assemble the bow, for other projects, stack the bow directly over the streamer, matching the pleated centres. If forming a double bow, add a second set of loops (about 2in (5cm) larger) before gluing to the streamer. Use the low temperature glue gun to stick them together and hold them tightly squeezed together. Use the hot glue to bond one short end of the connector piece to the underside of the gathered section of the streamer piece. Wrap the connector piece around the streamer piece and the bow loops two or three times. Glue the end of the connector piece to the underside of the bow and trim off any excess.

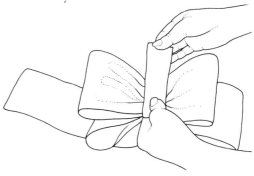

13 Open up the bow loops and arrange the streamers. Stuff the loops and scallops with plastic wrap to hold them in place until the fabric stiffener is dry. Trim the streamer ends to the desired length with a V-shaped notch.

14 When dry, seal and protect the stiffened bow and tails by painting on at least two layers of water-based glaze. This will dry clear and enhance the fabric with a deep lustre.

MAKING THE WREATH

15 To attach the stiffened bow to the French horn, place the gathered centre of the bow loops over the gathered centre of the streamer piece. Pinch together and, while holding these two pieces together with one hand, place into position on the French horn. Take the connector piece and use the glue gun to stick one

French horn wreath

end to the tubing of the French horn at the back of the bow. Wrap the connector piece around to the front of the bow. Continue wrapping it tightly around the bow and horn two or three times, finally gluing it to the back of the bow and trimming off any excess.

16 While holding the centre of the bow and the horn, open up the loops and stuff with soft plastic wrap to shape them.

17 Drape the bow tails and hold the scallops in place using the glue gun. Stuff the tail loops to hold the shape until dried. Trim back the streamer ends with a V-shaped notch.

18 To seal and protect the stiffened bow when dry, remove the stuffing and brush on two or three coats of water-based glaze, allowing it to dry between coats. You should aim to cover as much of the stiffened fabric as possible – back, front, underneath and inside loops and scallops. The glaze will dry clear.

19 Using florist's wire, attach small branches and pieces of fresh, preserved or silk fir to the French horn. I have used six pieces of fir about 6in (15cm) long with three pieces on each side of the bottom centre. Wire or glue on bunches of holly, sprigs of heather and various pine cones to create a lush fullness. The addition of a few sprigs of gypsophila will accent and lighten the final arrangement.

Table Setting

The tartan theme can be continued in the dining room to decorate the Christmas table. The rich, warm colours and bold plaid pattern of tartan make an ideal backdrop to a warming festive feast of roast turkey and Christmas pudding. In this section are included a wonderful golden swan centrepiece, decorated with a magnificent tartan bow, together with matching tartan serviette rings and Christmas crackers, all of which are very easy to make. If you so desired, you could even extend the theme further by laying the table with a tartan tablecloth and matching tartan serviettes.

SERVIETTE RINGS

MATERIALS

Scissors

1yd (90cm) fabric (makes 8-10 serviette rings)

Tape measure

Aluminium foil

Sticky tape

Fabric stiffener

Coat hanger and pegs

Low temperature glue gun and glue sticks

Soft plastic wrap, for stuffing

Water-based glaze

Paintbrush

1 For each serviette ring cut the following strips of fabric:
1 streamer piece – 4 x 10in (10 x 25cm);
1 bow loop piece – 4 x 12in (10 x 30cm);
1 ring piece – 4 x 6in (10 x 15cm);
1 connector piece – 2 x 6in (5 x 15cm).

2 Follow the instructions given for making a stiffened bow as in steps 2-11 on pages 49-50. Coat the ring piece with fabric stiffener and fold in the same way as the other strips.

3 Take the ring piece and form a circle with at least a ½in (12mm) overlap. Gather the overlapped section with three pleats, similar to the streamer and bow loop pieces. Hold in place with a peg.

4 To assemble, stack the bow loop piece over the streamer piece, matching the pleated centres. Glue together using the low temperature glue gun. Stack the bow and streamer piece over the ring piece and glue in place with hot glue. Glue one end of the connector piece to the inside of the ring piece, under the overlapping section of fabric. Tightly wrap the connector piece around all three layers (streamer, bow and ring) two or three times. Bond the connector piece to the inside of the ring piece with low temperature hot glue. Trim any remainder of the connector piece.

5 Open up the bow loops and stuff both the ring and bow loops with balls of stuffing. When dry, trim the streamers to the desired length, making a V-shaped notch.

6 When thoroughly dry, remove the stuffing and paint the bow with two layers of water-based glaze to seal and protect the fabric.

GOLDEN SWAN CENTREPIECE

MATERIALS

Papier mâché swan (available from craft shops)
Gold aerosol paint
Paintbrush
Gold acrylic paint
Scissors
1yd (90cm) Christmas tartan fabric, 45in (1.1m) wide
Tape measure
Water-based glaze
Aluminium foil
Sticky tape
Fabric stiffener
Coat hanger and pegs
Low temperature glue gun and glue sticks
Soft plastic wrap, for stuffing
Small pieces of fir
Sprigs of heather
Sprigs of gypsophila

1 In a well-ventilated area, spray the swan with two light coats of gold aerosol paint. Alternatively, use a paintbrush to paint the swan with two coats of gold acrylic paint.

2 Cut the fabric into three strips for the bow as follows:
1 streamer piece – 8 x 45in (20 x 112.5cm);
1 bow loop piece – 8 x 18in (20 x 45cm);
1 connector piece – 4 x 10in (10 x 25cm).

3 From the remaining fabric, cut out motifs to appliqué onto the swan. (Study the photograph on pages 52-53).

4 Using water-based glaze, stick the appliqué motifs into the desired position around the swan. Allow to dry, then brush on one or two coats of water-based glaze.

5 Make a bow following the instructions for making a stiffened bow as given in steps 2-14 on pages 49-50.

6 Glue the bow into position at the back of the swan with the tails furled out behind.

7 Glue small pieces of fresh, preserved or silk fir along the back of the swan so that they extend out from the bow, between the two furled tails. Add a few sprigs of heather and gypsophila to accent the arrangement.

TARTAN CRACKERS

MATERIALS

Recycled matt wrapping paper, 13½ x 8in (34 x 20cm)

Motto

Snap

Stiff card, 7 x 3¾in (17.5 x 9.5cm)

Tacky glue

2 formers (plastic piping, 2in (5cm) in diameter), 10in (25cm) long and 6in (15cm) long

Waxed cord

Party hat and small gifts

16in (40cm) tartan ribbon, 1½in (4cm) wide

1½yd (1.4m) gold-edged satin ribbon, ¼in (6mm) wide

1 Referring to the diagram on page 99 for placement, put the paper right side down on the work surface. Place a motto in the centre of the paper. Put the snap over the motto. Place the stiff card over the snap, but along the bottom edge. Spread glue along the top edge of the paper.

2 With the long former on the left and the short former on the right, butt the ends of the formers along the right-hand edge of the stiff card. Roll the paper around the formers, holding them together, until reaching the glued edge. Continue to roll over the glued edge. Wipe away excess glue and allow to dry.

3 Pull the short former on the right about ¾in (2cm) away from the right-hand edge of the stiff card ('pull line A' on the diagram). Wrap the waxed cord twice around the paper, centrally between the right-hand edge of the stiff card and the left-hand edge of the short former ('cord line A' on the diagram).

4 Pull the ends of the waxed cord in opposite directions, so the cord creases the paper around the edge of the stiff card. Push the short former back against the longer former and the card to shape the cracker. Remove the waxed cord, then the short former.

5 Drop into the remaining long tube a folded party hat, and a few little gifts. Carefully pull the long former to 'pull line B'. Make sure that the gifts drop into the cracker before closing the other end.

6 Wrap the cord twice around the paper at 'cord line B'. Pull the cord tightly as in step 4. Push the long former tube back against the stiff card. Remove the cord and the former.

7 Cut the tartan ribbon into two. Gather up each piece along one long edge to make a frill and tie one in each crease. Glue satin ribbon around the outside edges and in the central section. Tie two bows with the remaining satin ribbon; glue one over each tartan frill.

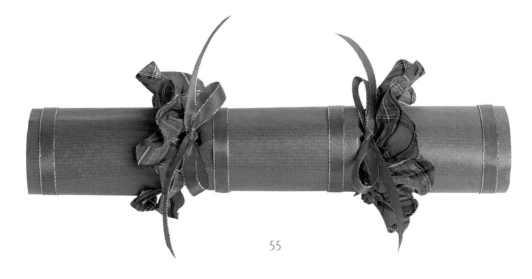

CHAPTER 4

A Toyland Theme

$\mathcal{P}$REPARING FOR CHRISTMAS can be particularly fun and satisfying when decorating the tree and home for younger family members. Children love to make things and have a special appreciation for handmade creations. Maybe the reason why adults love the seasonal preparations is because it reminds them of the wonderful time they had when they were children!

One of the nice things about our toyland theme is the ease with which it can be incorporated into any other theme - colour, country, Victorian, and so on. All you have to do is add toys and novelties to correspond with the particular theme. For example, in the country theme you could add corn dollies and miniature scarecrows. In the Victorian theme you might add small toys from that era, such as spinning tops and china dolls. It is so much fun to design and create this festive theme and the final result always delights young and old alike.

Tree Decorations

For the toyland tree I have chosen the basic Christmas colours of red, white and green. To light the tree I have used multicoloured miniature bulbs. Garlands of everlasting sweets swing from the tree boughs which are dotted with iced cookies and lollipops. Colourful hobby horses and dressed-up teddies guard the birthday cake candles in specially decorated spool holders which are for decoration only. Miniature parcels hint at the anticipated gift exchange on Christmas morning, when we all become kids at heart!

SWEETIE GARLAND

MATERIALS

The amount of materials required depends on the number and length of garlands you are making. The amounts given below will make one 25in (62.5cm) garland. For my tree I used eight garlands of this length.

16 squares of assorted fabric, 4 x 4in (10 x 10cm)
16 cotton wool balls
Dressmaking pins
32 lengths of wire, approximately 8in (20cm) long
Long-nosed pliers
32 lengths of ribbon, 10-12in (25-30cm) long, to co-ordinate with the fabric

1 Taking each square of fabric at a time, unravel two opposite edges to form a fringe about ¼ in (6mm) wide.

2 Place a fabric square on a work surface so that the wrong side is facing upwards and the fringed edges are on both the left- and right-hand sides.

3 Place a cotton wool ball at the bottom (non-fringed) edge of the fabric square, centrally between the two fringed edges. Fold ½ in (12mm) of the top edge of the fabric towards the cotton ball. Then roll the fabric along the bottom edge around the cotton ball towards the opposite non-fringed edge, to form a tube. Hold the fabric in place with a pin.

4 Wrap a piece of wire around each side of the cotton ball, approximately 1in (2.5cm) from each of the fringed edges. Wrap the wire around twice and pull tightly (using small long-nosed pliers can help with pulling the wire tight). Twist the two wires together two or three times to complete the sweet shape. Remove the pin. Repeat to make 15 more sweet shapes. Do not trim the wire.

5 Place the wired sections of two sweets over each other at an angle. Wrap and twist the excess wire around to the back (where the fold is) to attach them to each other. Repeat this process until you have 16 sweets attached in a garland chain.

6 Leave the wire on the two ends of the chain to attach the garland to the tree. Trim the remaining wires at the back of the garland chain and, using pliers, tuck the wire ends under the folded edge of the fabric.

7 Tie small ribbon bows with the lengths of ribbon and glue these over the wires showing at the front of the garland chain.

TREE SKIRT

An easy way of finishing off the area around the bottom of the tree is with a tree skirt. Plain fabric tree skirts can be purchased quite inexpensively; for instructions of how to make one, see page 88. Once the basic skirt is made, you can decorate it in many different ways. For the toyland tree skirt I used the same sweetie garland that is used on the tree. A chain of 86 sweet-like pieces are joined together in a chain which is then basted around a plain white tree skirt (making it easy to remove to wash or to alter the decoration).

Sweetie garland and wrapped lollipops

WRAPPED LOLLIPOP

MATERIALS

Measurements given are per lollipop and may need to be adjusted depending on the size of lollipop used.

Christmas fabric, 4½in (11.5cm) square
Tulle, 5½in (14cm) square
Lollipop
7-8in (17.5-20cm) 28-gauge craft wire
12in (30cm) satin ribbon

1 Unravel the threads along all the edges of the Christmas fabric square to form a fringe about ¼in (6mm) wide.

2 Place the fabric square down on a work surface with the wrong side facing. Place the tulle centrally over the fabric and place the lollipop in the centre of the tulle.

3 Pulling up the corners first, wrap the fabric around the lollipop, using wire to hold it in place around the lollipop stick. Leave 1½-2in (4-5cm) of the wire ends for attaching the lollipop to the tree branches.

4 Tie ribbon around the wire (leave wire ends to attach to tree) and tie a simple bow at the opposite side to the wire ends.

PARCEL ORNAMENTS

These delightful little boxes are so quick and easy to make and decorate that you will soon find yourself making dozens to adorn your tree each year (find the instructions on pages 97–98). For the toyland theme I have used red and green recycled paper with florist's ribbon curls to decorate the parcels.

Parcel ornaments and hobby horse

HOBBY HORSE

MATERIALS

Tracing paper
Pencil
Fabric A, 5 x 10in (12.5 x 25cm)
Fabric B, 11 x 3in (27.5 x 7.5cm)
Scissors
Felt, 2 x 3in (5 x 7.5cm)
Needle and cotton
Pins
25in (62.5cm) satin ribbon (in a co-ordinating colour),
$\frac{1}{8}$in (3mm) wide
5in (12.5cm) wooden dowel, $\frac{1}{4}$in (6mm) thick
Tacky glue
Wadding or toy stuffing
Strong thread
4 small buttons in colours to co-ordinate with fabric
2 large buttons

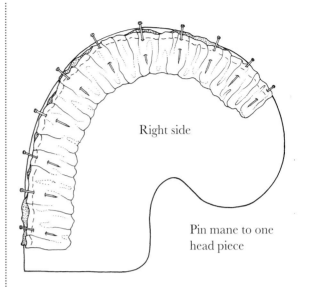

Right side

Pin mane to one
head piece

1 Trace the hobby horse head and ear patterns (see page 122). Position the head tracing over fabric A and cut out two pieces. Position the tracing of the ears over the felt and cut out two.

2 Fold fabric B in half lengthways, with right sides together, making it 11 x 1½in (27.5 x 4cm). Sew a ¼in (6mm) seam along the width at each end of the folded strip. Turn right side out and press. Sew a gathering stitch along the raw edges. Pull the gathering threads until the fabric measures approximately 5in (12.5cm). This will be the 'mane' piece.

3 Place one end of the mane piece ¼in (6mm) from the bottom outside edge of one head piece, right sides together. Pin the remainder of the mane piece along the out-side edge of that head piece (see the diagram).

4 With the right sides of the head pieces together, sew together (through the mane) leaving an ⅛in (3mm) seam allowance. Leave an opening at the bottom of the head, as indicated on the pattern.

5 Wrap satin ribbon in a spiral manner around the wooden dowel. Secure the ribbon at each end with a dab of glue.

6 Turn the head piece right side out and stuff it lightly with wadding. Place the dowel into the neck and continue stuffing around the dowel. Hand-stitch the bottom of the neck.

7 Fold one ear in half lengthways and over-sew the bottom edge. Repeat with the other ear. Stitch the ears into place on each side of the head.

8 Using very strong thread, stitch buttons to the head to form eyes. Pull the buttons in very tightly, to form small indentations.

9 Place satin ribbon around the nose and head to form the halter. Glue ribbon reins to the halter.

10 Glue one large button on each side of the bottom end of the dowel to form wheels. Glue a small button in the centre of each of the larger buttons.

SPOOLIE CANDLEHOLDER

MATERIALS

The amount of materials are approximate and are dependent on the size of spool used. Other colours of paint and ribbon may be used as desired.

Wooden cotton spools
White gloss acrylic paint
Paintbrush
Miniature clothes peg (available from craft shops and doll-making suppliers)
Green gloss acrylic paint
Tacky glue
15in (38cm) Christmas green satin ribbon, $1/16$in (1.5mm) wide
3in (7.5cm) Christmas red satin ribbon, $1/16$in (1.5mm) wide
2in (5cm) red rose trim
Low temperature hot glue gun and glue sticks
Red birthday cake candle
12in (30cm) white satin ribbon, $1/16$in (1.5mm) wide

1 Paint the cotton spool with white gloss acrylic paint, and paint the miniature clothes peg with green gloss acrylic paint. Allow to dry, then apply a second coat if necessary.

2 Using tacky glue, attach green ribbon around the top of the spool, red ribbon around the bottom of the spool and the red rose trim around the centre.

3 Almost fill the hole at the green ribbon end of the spool with hot glue and quickly attach a candle, holding it in place until the glue cools.

CAUTION: These candles and holders are for decoration only and under no circumstances should they be lit.

4 Tie a double bow with the white satin and remaining green satin ribbons, and glue it to the bottom of the candle where it enters the spool, using tacky glue.

5 Using hot glue, attach the miniature clothes peg to the bottom of the spool. This is to attach the candleholder to the tree.

SANTA'S TEDDY HELPER

MATERIALS

Scissors
Red felt, 4 x $3 1/2$in (10 x 9cm)
White felt, $1 1/2$ x 4in (4 x 10cm)
Tacky glue
Needle and thread
1 white pom-pom, $3/8$in (1cm) in diameter
2 red pom-poms, $3/8$in (1cm) in diameter
Jointed teddy bear, 4in (10cm) long
Red felt or ribbon, 8 x $1/4$in (20cm x 6mm)

1 Following the pattern given on page 122, cut out one hat pattern from the 4 x $3 1/2$in (10 x 9cm) piece of red felt. Cut the cuff pattern from the white felt.

2 Glue the white felt cuff piece to the bottom edge of the red felt hat piece, as indicated by the dotted line on the pattern.

3 Fold the hat in half lengthways, sew an $1/8$in (3mm) seam, turn inside out and press. Stitch a white pom-pom to the tip of the hat.

4 Place the hat over one ear of the teddy and stitch into place. Bend the hat down as shown in the photograph.

5 Sew a pom-pom to each end of the remaining piece of red felt. Tie this around the neck of the teddy to make a scarf.

WAISTCOAT TEDDY

MATERIALS

Tracing paper

Pencil

Scissors

Red or green felt, 8 x 4in (20 x 10cm)

Jointed teddy bear, 6in (15cm) long

3 very small buttons or $\frac{1}{8}$in (3mm) beads

Needle and thread

Tacky glue

Christmas fabric for bow tie

1 Trace the pattern given on page 123 and use this to cut out the waistcoat from the felt.

Carefully slit the armholes as marked. Cut one strip measuring $\frac{5}{8}$ x 2in (1.5 x 5cm) from the Christmas fabric.

2 Slip the felt waistcoat on to the teddy bear. Overlap the right side over the left by about $\frac{1}{4}$in (6mm). Stitch buttons or beads through both layers of the felt to close the waistcoat.

3 Tie a knot in the Christmas fabric strip; trim the ends to form a bow tie $\frac{3}{4}$in (2cm) long. Glue the bow tie under the teddy's chin; stick a button or bead over the knot.

Spoolie candleholder, Santa's teddy helper and waistcoat teddy

BISCUIT CUTTER ORNAMENTS

DOUBLE HEART BISCUIT CUTTER

MATERIALS

Tacky glue
28in (70cm) red dot satin ribbon, $\frac{3}{8}$in (1cm) wide
Large heart biscuit cutter
Small heart biscuit cutter
8in (20cm) red dot satin ribbon, $\frac{1}{8}$in (3mm) wide
Jingle bell, $\frac{1}{2}$in (12mm)
Scissors
1 red ribbon rose
Low temperature hot glue gun

1 Using tacky glue, attach the wider ribbon centrally around the side of each of the biscuit cutters. Trim the excess ribbon.

2 Thread the narrower ribbon through the bell. Glue the ribbon to the top of the small heart, allowing the bell to hang slightly inside the smaller heart. Trim the ribbon.

3 Using the narrower ribbon, form a small loop from the large heart to the small heart, allowing the small heart to hang from the larger heart. Glue the ribbon at the top of the larger heart. Trim the excess ribbon.

4 With the remaining narrower ribbon, make a hanging loop for the ornament, and glue it to the larger biscuit cutter.

5 Cut the remaining wider ribbon in half and form two figure-of-eight shapes. Place one over the top of the other at right angles and glue a ribbon rose in the centre. Glue this to the top of the ornament.

Opposite Double heart, tartan heart and star biscuit cutter ornaments, and iced cookies, see page 66

TARTAN HEART

MATERIALS

Tacky glue
1 medium heart biscuit cutter
7in (17.5cm) ribbon with tartan design, $\frac{3}{8}$in (1.5cm) wide
Jingle bell, $\frac{1}{2}$in (12mm)
5in (12.5cm) dark green satin ribbon, $\frac{1}{16}$in (1.5mm) wide
Low temperature hot glue gun and glue sticks
7in (17.5cm) red feather-edged satin ribbon, $\frac{1}{4}$in (6mm) wide
Small green button

1 Spread tacky glue evenly on the outside edge of the biscuit cutter. Starting at the top where the heart dips, place the tartan ribbon over the glue, all around the heart shape. Trim away any excess ribbon.

2 Thread the bell onto the narrow green ribbon and suspend it from the centre of the heart by making a loop. Use hot glue to attach the loop.

3 Tie a bow with the red feather-edged ribbon and glue it to the top of the heart. Finish by gluing a small button in the centre of the bow with tacky glue.

STAR BISCUIT CUTTER

MATERIALS

12in (30cm) red satin ribbon, $\frac{1}{8}$in (3mm) wide
Six-pointed star biscuit cutter (3in (7.5cm) from point to opposite point)
Tacky glue
12in (30cm) feather-edged red satin ribbon, $\frac{3}{8}$in (1cm) wide
Ribbon rose

1 Wrap the narrow red ribbon over the star cutter from one inside point (bottom of star

point) to the one directly opposite it. Take the ribbon over the edge and glue it about midway onto the side of the cutter. Repeat to wrap all inside points of the star. The ribbons will intersect in the centre.

2 Glue the feather-edged ribbon around the outside edge of the biscuit cutter, covering the ends of the narrow ribbon glued to the side.

3 To make a hanging loop, take 2-2⅛ in (5-7.5cm) of narrow red ribbon. Form this into a small loop and glue it to the outside edge of the cutter, in one of the dips between points.

4 Embellish the star ornament by gluing a ribbon rose over the centre, where all the narrow ribbons intersect.

ICED COOKIES

MATERIALS

Makes about 50 cookies depending on size.

6oz (185g/1½ cups) icing sugar
4oz (125g/1 cup) soft butter
Mixing bowl
Wooden spoon
1 teaspoon vanilla essence
½ teaspoon almond extract
1 egg
6oz (185g/1½) cups plain flour
1 teaspoon bicarbonate of soda
Rolling pin
Biscuit cutters
Skewer
Baking tray

Vanilla Icing:
12oz (375g/3 cups) icing sugar
1½oz (45g/⅓ cup) soft butter
1½ teaspoons vanilla essence
1-2 tablespoons milk
Food colouring (optional)

Wire rack
Palette knife
Lengths of ribbon (for hanging)

1 Cream together the icing sugar and butter in a mixing bowl. When well blended, add vanilla essence, almond extract and the egg and mix well. Slowly add the remaining ingredients, combining thoroughly. Leave the mixture to stand in the refrigerator for about four hours.

2 Preheat the oven to 180°C (350°F/Gas Mark 4). Roll out the dough to a thickness of ¼ in (6mm) and cut out the cookies using biscuit cutters. Make a small hole at the top of each cookie with a skewer (for threading through the hanging loop later). Bake on a tray for 6 to 8 minutes or until the edges are golden. Leave to cool on a wire rack

3 To make the vanilla icing, cream together the sugar and butter. Gradually stir in the vanilla essence and 1 tablespoon of milk, and combine thoroughly.

4 Add food colouring if desired. If necessary, add extra milk, one drop or two at a time, until the icing is smooth and spreadable.

5 When the cookies are cool, spread the icing over the tops of the cookies with a palette knife. Leave to set.

6 Thread a ribbon through the hole at the top of each cookie, knot the ends, and hang the iced cookies from the tree.

Room Decorations

Extend the festive toyland theme throughout the house by making some of the projects featured in this chapter. The toyland wreath greets visitors with a preview of the festive decorating theme used throughout the home to create a magical and exciting background to the anticipated festivities. The Christmas toyland stockings (seen on page 4) continue the theme in an endearing way. One stocking features Santa's cheery face, while the other is decorated with hobby horses, both of which will charm children of all ages.

The wreath (see page 68)

THE WREATH

MATERIALS

Sweetie Garland (see page 58)
Wreath
Florist's wire
White paper ribbon
3 Waistcoat Teddies (see page 63)

1 Weave one or two lengths of sweetie garland in and out all around the wreath. Fix the ends using small pieces of florist's wire. For extra security, attach garland to the fir branches at regular intervals with pieces of wire.

2 Make three single bows from the paper ribbon (see page 10). Attach the bows to the top of the wreath with wire.

3 Place three teddies around the wreath at regular intervals and secure in position with pieces of wire.

THE STOCKINGS

Gone are the days of using an old stocking from the drawer to hang on the fireplace or the end of the bed in anticipation of a nighttime visit from Father Christmas. Using felt and glue along with the endless choice of embellishments in the form of lace, ribbons, beads, sequins, and so on, it is both quick and easy to create a personalized stocking for children and adults alike (pictured on page 4).

For this toyland theme I have used the same Santa pattern as on the serviette rings (see page 69) as well as two hobby horses from the tree in a pocket to decorate the stockings. Other ideas you might consider could include a snowman, a Christmas wreath, snowflakes, stars, gingerbread people, soldiers or teddies. These could even be personalized with names or initials.

SANTA FACE STOCKING

MATERIALS

Fabric or pre-made stocking
Scissors
White felt, 8in (20cm) square
Red felt, 10in (25cm) square
Flesh-coloured felt, 5in (12.5cm) square
Tacky glue
2 round or oval eyes, $\frac{3}{8}$in (1.5cm) wide
$\frac{1}{4}$in (6mm) red pom-pom
$\frac{1}{2}$in (12mm) white pom-pom

1 Follow the instructions on page 46 to make a stocking. Follow the instructions for the serviette rings (see page 69) to make the Santa face, adding a felt hat made from a triangle of red felt folded in half and stitched along the edge.

2 Position the face onto the front of the stocking. Hand-stitch or use tacky glue to fix. Add a white pom-pom to the tip of the cap.

HOBBY HORSE STOCKING

MATERIALS

Fabric or pre-made stocking
Scissors
Fabric for pocket
Needle and thread
2 Hobby Horses (see page 61)

1 Follow the instructions on page 46 to make a stocking. Then cut out the pocket pattern given on page 122 from your chosen fabric. Turn under the cut edges of the pocket $\frac{1}{4}$in (6mm) and press.

2 Position the pocket on the stocking. Stitch around the sides and bottom of the pocket.

3 Position one hobby horse peeping out of the pocket, and the other in front of pocket. Baste down to secure.

Table Setting

The Christmas toyland table captures the fun and merriment of this festive theme. It is dominated by a wonderful cracker centrepiece, a giant cracker that has seemingly just been pulled, with sweets and gifts cascading around. To add to the jollity, Santa's beaming face smiles up from every serviette ring. With such cheerful table decorations, who could fail to enjoy their Christmas fare?

SANTA SERVIETTE RINGS

MATERIALS

Scissors

White felt, 12in (30cm) square

Flesh-coloured felt, 5in (12.5cm) square

Red felt, 2in (5cm)

Tacky glue

2 x ¾ in (2cm) round or oval eyes

¼ in (6mm) red pom-pom

Red paper serviette

1 Referring to patterns on page 124, cut out the following pieces from white felt: beard and hair piece, fur piece, moustache and serviette ring strip. Cut out the face from flesh-coloured felt, and cheeks and mouth from red felt.

2 Assemble the face by first placing the white beard and hair felt piece flat on the work surface. Refer to the table setting photograph on pages 70–71 for the positioning of the various felt pieces. Glue the flesh-coloured face into position. Glue the fur piece over the hair and flesh-coloured face. Glue the moustache into place, leaving openings for inserting the cheeks and mouth. Glue the cheeks and mouth into place and glue the sections of moustache over them. Glue the eyes and pom-pom nose into position.

3 Refer to the diagram for making the ring which holds the serviette. Start by laying the white felt piece down on the work surface. Fold the serviette in a cone shape and lay it over the centre of the felt strip. Fold the ends of the felt strip around the serviette and glue where they intersect.

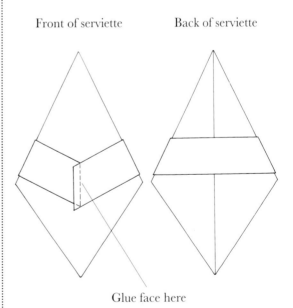

Front of serviette   Back of serviette

Glue face here

4 Glue the Santa face over the serviette ring where the two ends meet. The top part of the serviette forms the hat. Santa's beard should cover the bottom section of the serviette.

CRACKER CENTREPIECE

MATERIALS

Scissors

Thin card, 21 x 16in (52.5 x 40cm)

Tacky glue

Water

Wrapping paper or fabric, 29 x 18in (72.5 x 45cm)

Glue brush

2¼yd (2m) ribbon, ⅛in (3mm) wide

Curling or florist's ribbon for decoration

Ribbon shredder

Shredded paper

Sweets and presents for decoration

1 Cut the thin card into three pieces, each measuring 7 x 16in (17.5 x 40cm). Thin the glue by adding water in the proportion of 1 part water to 2 parts glue.

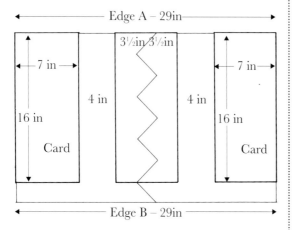

2 Lay the paper or fabric down on a flat surface with the wrong side facing. Brush a light layer of thin glue over one side of each card piece, working with one piece at a time. Position the card over the wrong side of the paper or fabric, as shown in the diagram.

3 When the thin glue has dried, cut down the centre of the middle piece of card in a zigzag fashion.

4 Working on one side of the cracker at a time, brush undiluted tacky glue along the paper and about 1in (2.5cm) of the card along edge B. Roll edge A towards edge B, overlapping the glue by about 1in (2.5cm). Smooth the paper and hold it in place until dry. Trim the zigzag edge to make it blend in where the card overlaps itself. Repeat with the other half of the cracker.

5 Wrap 40in (1m) of ribbon twice around the centre of the 4in (10cm) wrapping paper gap of one half of the cracker. Then pull the

ribbon until the paper creases and the card edges touch. Tie the ribbon in a knot but do not trim the ribbon tails (these will be used to attach the ribbon curls later). Repeat with the other half of the cracker.

6 Take ten 18in (45cm) strips of curling ribbon and tie them tightly in the gap between the cracker sections. To curl the ribbon, hold one strip of ribbon at a time, as close to the central knot as possible, between your thumb and the sharp edge of a pair of scissors. Pull your thumb and scissor blade firmly to the end of the strip to form a curl. Repeat, holding the strip even tighter if a tighter curl is preferred. Before going on to the next strip of ribbon, use a ribbon shredder to make the curls thinner, giving them a frothy look. Curl and shred the ends of ribbon which formed the knot.

7 Place both cracker halves in the centre of the table. Fill with shredded paper and arrange sweets and presents to look as if the cracker has just been pulled and everything is tumbling out.

CHAPTER 5

A Scandinavian Theme

CHRISTMAS IN SCANDINAVIA began as a pagan holiday which was celebrated around January 13 for three days and nights. It was in the early 1800s that the mixture of Scandinavian tradition and German custom began to form today's celebration.

The festivities begin on Christmas Eve and continue over the next two days with a variety of local customs and traditions. Reciting the Christmas story and singing carols around the tree are as much a part of any Scandinavian Christmas as the festive meals.

Long winter evenings provide time to create the decorations which form the basis of the various seasonal customs. Woven hearts, sheaves of wheat, beautiful embroidered linens and a profusion of lit candles (recreated here with electric candle lights) join the snow white and rosy warm red festive colours to create that special glow of a Scandinavian Christmas welcome.

Tree Decorations

Focal to the tree is the traditional flag garland which runs vertically and includes flags from Norway, Sweden and Denmark. Electric candle lights illuminate the customary tree decorations, which include flower-filled Julekurv (woven hearts), colourful woven stars, sheaves of wheat and friendly Julenisser (elves). The fragrant gingerbread hearts, together with the freshness of the Norwegian spruce, produce the time-honoured smells of a Scandinavian Christmas.

FLAG GARLAND

While most households would use only the flags from one country on their garland, we have chosen to include the flags from Norway, Sweden and Denmark to give a more general Scandinavian flavour.

MATERIALS

The amount of felt and ribbon is enough for a length of garland 20in (50cm) long. Measure the height of your tree to determine how many lengths you require, and the amount of materials required.

Scissors
76in (190cm) white satin ribbon, ¼in (6mm) wide
Bright red felt, 3 x 5½in (7.5 x 14cm)
Tape measure
Medium blue felt, 3 x 2¾in (7.5 x 7cm)
9in (22cm) navy blue satin ribbon,
⅛in (3mm) wide
28in (70cm) yellow satin ribbon, ¼in (6mm) wide
20in (50cm) red satin ribbon, ¼in (6mm) wide
Tacky glue

1 Cut six strips of white ribbon, long enough to run from the top to the bottom of the tree.

2 For every 20in (50cm) of white ribbon, cut four red and two blue rectangles of felt, each measuring 2¾ x 1½in (7 x 4cm). These will make six flags, two from each country.

3 Referring to the diagrams below, make the following Scandinavian flags:

Norwegian Taking a red felt rectangle, glue a 2¾in (7cm) strip of white ribbon along the centre of the length of the rectangle. Glue a 1½in (4cm) strip of white ribbon along the centre of the width of the rectangle. Glue a strip of navy ribbon along the centre of the length and width of the white ribbon already in place.

Danish Taking a red felt rectangle, glue a 2¾in (7cm) strip of white ribbon along the centre of the length of the rectangle. Glue a 1½ in (4cm) strip of white ribbon along the centre of the width of the rectangle.

Swedish Taking a medium blue felt rectangle, glue a 2¾in (7cm) strip of yellow ribbon along the centre of the length of the rectangle. Glue a 1½in (4cm) strip of yellow ribbon along the centre of the width of the rectangle.

4 For each 20in (50cm) of the garland, cut two 8in (20cm) lengths each of yellow, red and white ribbon. Tie them in bows, measuring 1½–2in (4–5cm) across the loops.

5 Glue on one yellow bow at the top end of the long white ribbon strip. Glue a Danish flag ¾in (2cm) down from the yellow bow. Glue a white bow ¾in (2cm) from the bottom of the flag. Glue a Norwegian flag ¾in (2cm) down from the white bow. Glue a red bow ¾in (2cm) from the bottom of the flag. Glue a Swedish flag ¾in (2cm) down from the red bow. Repeat the pattern to the end of the strip of white ribbon. Repeat with the remaining strips of white ribbon.

6 Wedge all the ribbon bows between the tree branches.

JULENISSER

These small characters are the Scandinavian's version of Santa's helpers (or elves). It was the practice in olden days to put a bowl of *Grøt* (a rice pudding) out in the barn on Christmas Eve. Of course, to this day one can never be sure who exactly eats the *Grøt* – the *Julenisser* or the neighbourhood boys!

MATERIALS

Scissors

Stiff card

Tape measure

Bright red 4-ply yarn (3½oz/100g makes 14 *nisser*)

Flesh-coloured felt, 3½ x 1½in (9 x 4cm)

Red felt, 4⅜ x 4¾in (11 x 12cm) per *nisser*

Needle and cotton

Tacky glue

Cotton wool

Pair of ⅛in (3mm) boggle eyes

White satin ribbon, ¼in (6mm) wide (approximately 40in (1m) per *nisser*, 8in (20cm) per bow)

Small gold bell

1 Cut two pieces of stiff card, each measuring 6 x 4in (15 x 10cm). Wrap red yarn around the length of one piece of card 20 times (to form 20 loops). Tie off the yarn ¾in (2cm) from each end. This will form the arms.

2 To make the body, wrap red yarn around the second piece of stiff card to form 40 loops.

75

3 Tie red yarn around all 40 loops of yarn, 3¼in (8cm) from one end and 2¾in (7cm) from the other end. Divide the 3¼in (8cm) length in half to form the legs. Tie red yarn around each leg, ¾in (2cm) from the end.

4 Thread the arms through the yarn loops at the other end, bringing them down to the thread around the top of the legs. Tie red yarn around the body, 1½in (4cm) from the other end of the yarn loops.

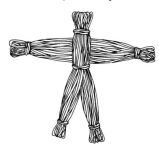

5 Glue the flesh-coloured felt around the head section of the yarn loops.

6 Cut out two triangular pieces of red felt and sew the sides together to make the hat. Glue this on the felt head.

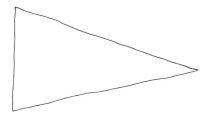

7 Gently shape a cotton ball to form hair and a beard. Glue these into position on the head. Glue the boggle eyes to the face.

8 Glue small white bows on the tied-off sections of the arms and legs, and sew a small gold bell to the top of the hat. Make a hanging loop from white ribbon and glue or stitch the ends to the hat.

WOVEN STARS

MATERIALS

The instructions given are for the smaller star. Adjust the measurements to make larger variations.

Scissors
Red and white floristry ribbon, ⅝in (1.5cm) wide
Needle and clear thread
Auto-fade pen

1 Cut four strips of ribbon 18½in (46cm) long. Fold each strip in half and cut the ends at a 45° angle. Using an auto-fade pen, mark one end of each strip with a number (1-4) and the other end with that number and letter 'a'.

2 Carefully refer to the diagrams shown below. With the 'a' sides facing away from you, hang strip 2 over the folded strip 1.

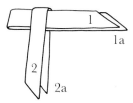

3 Turn the strips anti-clockwise so that the loop of strip 1 is pointing towards you. Now hang strip 3 over the double strip 2.

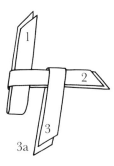

4 Turn the strips anti-clockwise again and hang strip 4 over the folded strip 3. Thread the ends through the folded end of strip 1 to form a square.

5 Carefully pull the strips together to close and neaten the square.

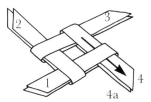

6 Fold strip 4 back across the centre to lie beside strips 2 and 2a. Repeat with strips 3, then strip 2, then strip 1. Tuck strip 1 underneath strip 4 to secure it in position and pull firmly.

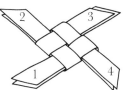

7 Fold strip 1 under and at right angles to lie next to strip 4a. Fold it at right angles again to lie beside strip 1a, across strips 4a and 2.

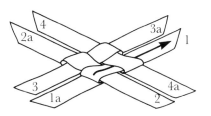

8 Fold this strip back on itself towards the centre so that triangle B lies on top of triangle A. Tuck the end through the fold underneath. Repeat with strips 2, 3 and 4. Turn the star over and repeat with strips 1a, 2a, 3a and 4a.

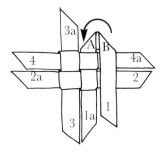

Sheaves of wheat and woven stars

9 Turn the star back to the other side. Bend but do not fold or crease, strip 1 under itself at right angles until it lies over strip 2a. Hold strip 4 to the side and bend strip 1 over itself towards the centre and slip it under strip 4 to lie over strip 4a. Pull it firmly to make a cone shape. Repeat with strip 2 until it lies over strip 1a. Repeat with strips 3 and 4.

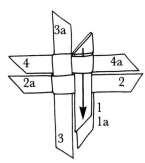

10 Turn the star over and repeat with strips 1a, 2a, 3a and 4a. Snip off any long ends so that they lie evenly with the star shape.

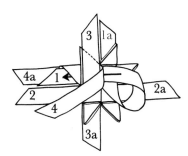

11 Thread the needle with clear thread and stitch a hanging loop at one corner of the star.

SHEAVES OF WHEAT

One of the oldest Scandinavian traditions still practised today is the fastening of a sheaf of oats to any structure in the garden for the enjoyment of the birds. Not only does this provide the birds with a welcome treat among the tons of snow, but it also offers hours of pleasure for bird watchers! In this variation on the traditional decoration, I have used wheat instead of oats.

MATERIALS
(per sheaf)
7 stalks of wheat, 8in (20cm) long
Florist's wire
12in (30cm) red satin ribbon, ¼in (6mm) wide
Tacky glue

1 Arrange the wheat stalks so that they form a triangular shape, with the central sheaf standing upright and three stalks leaning towards it on the right and left sides.

2 Wire the seven stalks together just at the base of the grain. Leave 2in (5cm) of wire free to attach the sheaf to the tree.

3 Tie a bow with the red satin ribbon and glue this over the wire at the front of the wheat sheaf.

TREE-TOP WREATH

MATERIALS
The amount of ribbon you need will depend on the distance the wreath must hang from the ceiling to the top of the tree. Adjust to suit personal measurements.

Tape measure
Straw wreath
Scissors
4½yd (4m) red satin ribbon, ⅜in (1.5cm) wide
Felt-tip pen
Tacky glue
Red thread
Large straw angel
4 small straw angels
4 straw stars

1 Measure the distance the wreath will hang from the ceiling. Double this measurement. Measure around the thickness of the straw wreath. Double this measurement and add to the previous measurement. Cut two lengths of ribbon this length.

2 Using a felt-tip pen, mark the straw wreath into quarters. Take the cut end of one long strip of ribbon and wrap it around one mark on the wreath. Take the other cut end of the same ribbon strip and wrap it around the mark at the opposite side of the wreath. Glue the ribbon ends to secure. Repeat with the other long piece of ribbon around the remaining felt-tip marks on the wreath.

Tree-top wreath

3 Tie four ribbon bows and glue these over the join where the ribbon strips wrap around the straw wreath.

4 Take a 20in (50cm) length of ribbon and tie a bow around the two loops about 2in (5cm) from the top.

5 Tie red cotton to the angels and stars. Hang the large angel from the bow at the top centre so that it dangles a little way below the middle of the straw wreath. Position the stars to hang from the ribbon surrounding the straw wreath. Place the small angels to hang below the straw wreath, centrally between the straw stars.

WOVEN BASKET

Traditionally made from red and white paper or felt, these charming heart-shaped woven baskets, or *Julekurv*, usually hold sweets when hung on the Christmas tree. For a light, feathery effect, I have filled this *Julekurv* with small bunches of gypsophila instead of the traditional sweets. On the festive Scandinavian table (see page 82) these woven baskets also serve as napkin holders, each with a little treat hidden at the bottom.

MATERIALS

White felt, 9 $^{1}/_{2}$ x 3in (24 x 7.5cm)
Red felt, 9 $^{1}/_{2}$ x 3in (24 x 7.5cm)
Tacky glue
Red felt, 9 $^{1}/_{2}$ x $^{3}/_{4}$ in (24 x 2cm)
Flowers or sweets to fill basket

1 Fold the piece of white felt in half and cut it according to the pattern given on page 123. Repeat with the larger piece of red felt.

2 Weave the felt strips as illustrated opposite to make the basket.

3 Glue the narrow strip of red felt to opposite sides of the inside centre of the top of the woven heart. Fill it with flowers or sweets as desired.

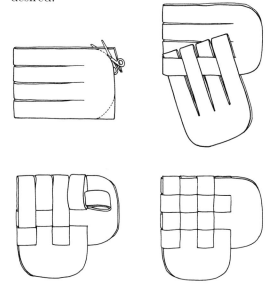

PEPPERKAKER

GINGERBREAD COOKIES

Tradition has it that to be a good Scandinavian housewife, one must make seven varieties of Christmas cookies. *Pepperkaker* is one such cookie. Made with ground ginger, and black pepper for that special 'kick', it is a delicious snack and is often used to make gingerbread houses and tree ornaments.

MATERIALS

3 $^{1}/_{2}$ oz (100g) light syrup
3 teaspoons powdered cinnamon
$^{1}/_{2}$ teaspoon ground black pepper
2 teaspoons ground cloves
1 $^{1}/_{2}$ teaspoons ground ginger
Small saucepan
Wooden spoon
8oz (250g) butter
6 $^{1}/_{2}$ oz (200g) sugar
Mixing bowl
1 egg

14oz (450g) plain flour

1 ½ teaspoons bicarbonate of soda

Rolling pin

Biscuit cutters

Skewer

Baking sheet

Wire rack

Icing:

1 egg white

1–2 teaspoons white vinegar

Icing sugar

Food colouring (optional)

Knife

Lengths of ribbon for hangers

1 Heat the syrup and spices in a small saucepan, stirring until the mixture begins to boil. Allow to cool.

2 Cream the butter and sugar in a mixing bowl. Add the syrup mixture and the egg.

3 Slowly stir in the flour and bicarbonate of soda. Mix to a smooth dough. Cover and keep cool in the refrigerator overnight.

Gingerbread cookies

4 Roll out the dough to a thickness of $^1/_8$–$^1/_4$ in (3-6mm). Using biscuit cutters, cut the dough into heart shapes of varying sizes. Make a small hole at the top of each heart with a skewer (for threading through the hanger later).

5 Bake on a floured baking sheet at 200°C (400°F/Gas Mark 6) for 5 to 8 minutes. Leave to cool on a wire rack.

6 When the cookies have cooled, make the icing by mixing together the egg white and white vinegar. Then add icing sugar until you achieve the consistency of custard. Food colouring can be added if desired. Carefully spread the icing on the cookies with a knife. Leave to harden.

7 Thread a ribbon through the hole at the top of each heart to make a hanging loop, knot the ends securely, and hang the *pepperkaker* from the tree.

Table Setting

In Scandinavia the festivities begin on Christmas Eve. In Norway, the day starts with a special raisin bread eaten in the morning, while Father puts a sheaf of wheat outside the kitchen window for the birds. After a simple lunch, younger Scandinavian children are sent to bed while the older ones go skiing. During this time, the parents decorate the tree. The children wake to ringing church bells and the magical tree in the late afternoon, when the family gather to read the Christmas story and say a blessing for the feast that follows, which includes such traditional dishes as Rømmegrøt, *a sour cream porridge with cinnamon and sugar, and seven different varieties of cookie.*

This Scandinavian table is draped with gorgeous hand-embroidered linen using a traditional Christmas theme. Greenery and candles surround the crowning Kransekake *or garland cake of our Scandinavian table, decorated in customary style with miniature flags.* Julekurv *placed on the dinner plates hold the serviettes, in addition to a tiny gift which pops out as the napkin is removed.*

GARLAND CAKE

This is a traditional cake used at all special occasions in Scandinavia such as Christmas, weddings and anniversaries.

MATERIALS

15oz (470g) almonds

Saucepan

Water

Food processor

10½oz (330g) icing sugar

2 egg whites

Aluminium foil

6½–9½oz (200–300g) marzipan

Rolling pin

Pencil

Baking parchment

Ruler

Glaze:

1 egg white

6½oz (200g) icing sugar

2-3 drops clear vinegar

Piping bag

Miniature flags and crackers for decoration

1 Plunge half of the almonds into boiling water for 30 seconds to loosen the skins and blanch them.

2 Place all the almonds in a food processor and grind coarsely. Add the icing sugar to the processor and grind the mixture to a fine consistency.

3 Add the egg whites and mix for 30 seconds at a medium speed, then another 30 seconds at the highest speed. The mixture should now form a dough.

4 Wrap this dough in a piece of aluminium foil and place in a cold oven. Set the oven at 100°C (200°F/Gas Mark ¼). Leave the dough in the oven for 1 hour.

5 Allow the dough to cool to body temperature. Gradually work the marzipan into the dough with your hands. Roll the dough into 'sausage' shapes of finger thickness.

6 Draw out 16 circles on the baking parchment. The smallest circle should be 1½in (4cm) in diameter. Each circle should be increased by ½in (1cm) up to the largest, which will be 7½in (19 cm) in diameter. (Alternatively, special baking tins can be purchased from Scandinavian speciality shops.)

7 Bake at 200°C (400°F/Gas Mark 6) for 8 to 10 minutes. Cool the rings quickly. The rings can be frozen or stored in an airtight container with a piece of bread (to prevent them from drying out). Place sufficient 'sausage' shapes of dough around the edge of each parchment circle to form a ring.

8 Mix up the glaze to a runny consistency. Place the largest ring on a plate. Pipe the glaze onto the ring in a zig-zag pattern, starting at the top of the ring. Place the next sized ring on top; the glaze will anchor it. Repeat with each successively smaller ring to form a tower.

9 Decorate the garland cake with miniature flags and crackers. When cutting the cake to eat it, remove the largest ring and cut that first to maintain the tower shape.

Opposite *Despite the long cold winter days and nights, Scandinavian homes reflect a cosy atmosphere with the introduction of rich bright reds to warm the stark white and natural tones they favour. This inviting window sends a warm welcome to family and friends, as well as passing strangers, with its display of woven stars and dangling night lights and profuse array of glowing candles.*

CHAPTER 6

A Victorian Theme

*I*T WAS DURING THE LAST CENTURY that
the festive custom of decorating an evergreen tree inside the home was introduced.
The Victorians had very little money to
spend on extravagant decorations yet they
were enthusiastic in their celebration of the
Christmas season, adapting
customs from other eras and countries.

The Victorian middle classes placed great
emphasis on the family. Family members
spent a lot of time designing and creating
personal gifts for each other, a tradition that
even extended to special household ser-
vants. They spent long, happy hours together, planning and creating decorations for
the tree and home. Their love of laces,
satins, ribbons and exotic flourishes were
reflected in this preparation for what
became a very special season.

In this chapter are featured many typical
Victorian decorations you can make for the
tree, the table and the home, enabling you
to recreate a Victorian Christmas.

Tree Decorations

In Victorian times, small lit candles would have made the tree glow at night. Nowadays, for safety reasons, we use miniature electric lights in the shape of small white candles to light an evergreen tree, enhancing its lush and glistening array of decorations.

TREE SKIRT

MATERIALS

Scissors
1¾yd (1½m) velvet fabric, 44in (1.1m) wide
2¼yd (2m) lace-covered satin fabric, 44in (1.1m) wide
14yd (12½m) insertion cord
Needle and cotton

1 Place a 25in (64cm) paper square down flat. Tie a pencil to one end of a 30in (75cm) length of string. Measure from bottom left corner, along bottom edge and make a mark at 5in (13cm). Repeat from bottom left corner, now going up left edge.

2 Take loose ends of the string in your left hand and the pencil in your right. Place the string along bottom edge of paper square. Put the pencil on the 5in (13cm) mark, and trap loose end of string under your thumb, keeping it taut over bottom left corner. You can check first by swinging string in an arc across the paper, to make sure the pencil will pass through both marks. When satisfied, mark out the arc. Repeat this process for the 25in (64cm) mark (the arc will cross from bottom right to top left corners). Cut out along the two arcs. Fold in half and cut along folded edge. Use these segment patterns to cut four velvet and four satin pieces allowing ¼in/6mm all around for seam allowances.

3 With right sides together, take one pattern piece each of velvet and lace-covered satin. Insert insertion cord and sew along edge, leaving ¼in (6mm) seam allowance.

4 Join the remaining six segments in the same way, alternating between satin and velvet, ensuring that cord is inserted between each segment. Do *not* sew up the last seam to make a continuous circle; instead leave a gap. Sew cord along one side of gap only. Baste insertion cord to the right side of the fabric around the outside edge.

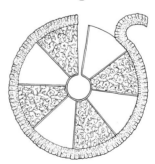

5 Take a strip of lace-covered satin 5in (12.5cm) wide and about 16ft (4.8m) long. Turn under one long edge about ¼in (6mm) and hem. Run gathering stitch along the other long edge. Pull up gathers and attach fabric to outside edge of the skirt, with right sides together, under the insertion cord.

6 Stitch under top edge of tree skirt; press.

BASKET ANGEL

MATERIALS

Wicker angel shape

Gold aerosol paint

Needle and cotton

Cream or ivory lace – the amount depends on the size
of wicker angel used. For this angel we used:

24in (60cm) flat lace, 4in (10cm) wide

15in (38cm) gathered lace, ½in (12mm) wide

10in (25cm) flat or gathered lace, 1in
(2.5cm) wide

Low temperature glue gun and glue sticks

30in (75cm) fused pearls

30in (75cm) gold cord

Ribbon roses

Ribbon

1 In a well-ventilated area, spray the wicker
angel shape with two mistings of gold paint.

2 Run two lines of gathering stitches along
the top edge of the wide flat lace. Pull the
stitches up to gather the lace and place it
around the wicker angel, just under the
wings. Tie the threads at the back to form a
high-waisted skirt. Secure the gathered edge
to the wicker angel with hot glue.

3 Glue the ½in (12mm) wide gathered lace
to the back of the wings, along the outside
edge. Glue fused pearls and gold cord over
the lace heading just glued to the back of
the wings. Glue fused pearls and
gold cord to the front of the

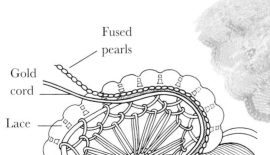

Fused
pearls

Gold
cord

Lace

wings, along the edge of where the lace
emerges.

4 Take the 1in (2.5cm) wide lace and cut it
into two pieces, one for each sleeve. Stitch a
row of gathering stitches along the inside
edge and pull tight to form a circle. Form this
circle into a sleeve by flattening it into a cone
shape. Glue the gathered edge to the wicker
arms, just above the top edge of the lace skirt.

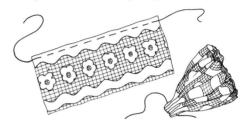

5 Glue a posy of ribbon roses behind and
around the hands. This will look like the angel
is carrying a bouquet while, at the same time,
covering the skirt and sleeve lace edges. Tie a
ribbon bow with long tails and glue it to the
bottom of the posy.

VICTORIAN FAN

MATERIALS

1yd (90cm) fine wire braid

12in (30cm) stiff flat lace, 3–3½in (7.5–9cm) wide

Low temperature glue gun and glue sticks

Florist's wire

1 small tassel

8in (20cm) thin gold cord

Hair spray

Ultra-fine gold glitter

1yd (90cm) burgundy satin ribbon, ⅛in (3mm) wide

Gypsophila

1 ribbon rosebud

1 Thread 12in (30cm) of the wire braid through the top edge of the stiff flat lace. Fold the lace concertina-fashion and pinch it together at the bottom edge. Glue the cut edges of the lace down and wrap florist's wire around the bottom edge to secure.

2 Glue or wire the tassel to the bottom edge. Thread a 5in (12.5cm) piece of thin gold cord through the lace in the centre top of the fan. Form a loop by knotting the two ends.

3 Spray the lace lightly with hair spray and, while still damp, sprinkle it very lightly with ultra-fine gold glitter. Spray again lightly to set. Allow the lace to dry well before shaking off the excess glitter.

4 Make a triple loop bow, 3in (7.5cm) wide, from the burgundy ribbon and wrap florist's wire around the centre to secure. Make a triple loop bow, 2in (5cm) wide, from the remaining fine wire braid.

5 Glue the burgundy ribbon bow over the wired bottom edge of the fan. Glue a small amount of gypsophila over the ribbon bow. Next stick the fine wire braid bow over the gypsophila and finish by gluing the ribbon rosebud in the centre of the gold bow.

CORNUCOPIA

MATERIALS

Decorative wrapping paper, 5 x 10in

(12.5 x 25cm)

Tacky glue

Tracing paper

Pencil

Scissors

Low temperature glue gun and glue sticks

12in (30cm) heavy wire gold cord

1yd (90cm) white satin ribbon, ⅛in (3mm) wide

Florist's wire

12in (30cm) gold grosgrain ribbon, ⅛in (3mm) wide

1 ribbon rose bow

Needle

12in (30cm) thin gold cord

Gypsophila

3 dried burgundy rosebuds

1 Fold the wrapping paper in half to form a 5in (12.5cm) square with the decorated side facing outwards. Glue the underside of the paper and seal the square closed. Allow to dry.

2 Trace the cornucopia pattern (page 123) on to one side of the square; cut it out. Roll it into a cone shape, overlapping the paper slightly at the front and secure with glue.

3 Starting at the top of the cone, at the front where the seam is, glue a length of heavy wire gold cord around the top edge. Glue another piece of cord over the seam, placing the edge of the cord at the top of the cone and running it down, 2in (5cm) past the bottom point.

4 Wrap a small piece of ribbon around the bottom point of the cord and paper cone to secure. Unravel the 2in (5cm) of cord hanging below the point to create a tassel effect.

Opposite *Victorian fan and cornucopia*

5 Make a triple loop bow with the white satin ribbon, leaving 3in (7.5cm) tails. Using florist's wire, wire the bow in the centre to secure and glue to the top front of the cone. Form a single loop collar bow from the gold ribbon and glue it over the white bow. Glue a white ribbon rose bow over the top.

6 Use a needle to thread the length of thin gold cord through the paper at the back of the cone. Tie the two ends together to form a loop.

7 Fill the paper cone with gypsophila and small dried burgundy rosebuds.

HOBBY HORSE

MATERIALS

Tracing paper

Pencil

Burgundy satin, 5 x 10in (12.5 x 25cm)

Flat lace, 5 x 10in (12.5 x 25cm)

Scissors

Needle and cotton

7–8in (17.5–20cm) ribbon, ⅛in (3mm) wide

5in (12.5cm) wooden dowel painted gold,

¼in (6mm) thick

Tacky glue

Wadding or toy stuffing

2 faceted beads, 4mm

Strong thread

14in (35cm) gathered lace, 1in (2.5cm) wide

14in (35cm) cream fused pearls

20in (50cm) gold cord

Ribbon, ribbon roses and beads for decoration

1 Trace the hobby horse head and ear patterns (page 122). Position the tracing over the satin and cut out two pieces of satin and two pieces of flat lace for the head and two of each for the ears.

2 Place the lace over the right side of the satin and sew the head pieces together (right side of lace-topped fabric together), leaving an opening at the bottom.

3 Wrap the ribbon in a spiral manner around the wooden dowel. Secure at each end with a dab of glue.

4 Turn the head right side out and stuff it lightly with wadding. Place the dowel into the centre of the neck opening and continue stuffing around the dowel. Hand-stitch the bottom of the neck to secure.

5 Place the lace ear over the satin ear and glue them together to prevent the satin from fraying. Fold one ear in half lengthways and oversew the bottom edge. Repeat with the other ear. Stitch the ears into place on either side of the head.

6 Stitch the beads to the head to form eyes. Use strong thread to pull the beads in tightly, forming small indentations.

7 Starting from in between the ears, hand-stitch or glue the gathered lace down the outside seam of the head to form the mane. Glue or stitch fused pearls along the edge of the lace where it attaches to the head.

8 Place gold cord around the nose and around the head to form the halter. Attach cord reins to the cord halter.

9 Decorate your hobby horse with ribbon, ribbon roses and beads. Have fun creating your own design.

PARASOL

MATERIALS

5in (12.5cm) wooden dowel, ¼in (6mm) wide

Gold acrylic paint

Paintbrush

8in (20cm) burgundy ribbon, ⅛in (3mm) wide

Tacky glue or low temperature glue gun and

glue sticks

Scissors

Ivory or cream net, 6in (15cm) square

Burgundy moiré fabric, 6in (15cm) square

24in (60cm) ivory or cream lace, ½in (12mm) wide

Tissue paper

Florist's wire

9in (22.5cm) burgundy ribbon, ¼in (6mm) wide

5in (12.5cm) burgundy ribbon, ¹⁄₁₆in (1.5mm) wide

1 Paint the wooden dowel with gold paint and allow to dry. Paint a second coat if required. Wrap ⅛in (3mm) wide ribbon

around the dowel in a spiral manner. Secure the ends with glue.

2 At one end of the dowel form a small ribbon loop. Cover the ends of the loop with a piece of ribbon wrapped around the end of the wooden dowel.

3 Cut a 5½ in (14cm) circle out of both the net and the moiré fabric. Glue lace around the outside edge of the net only.

4 To find the exact centre of the moiré fabric circle, fold it in half, then into quarters. Crease the folds slightly to mark the centre point. Lay the net circle on a work surface with the wrong side facing up. Lay the moiré fabric directly over the net with the wrong side facing up.

Hobby horse and parasol

5 Dab some glue at the centre point of the moiré fabric and place the bottom end of the dowel (without a ribbon loop) over that point, so the dowel is vertical. Mould some tissue paper around the bottom half of the dowel.

6 Bring the fabric and net over the tissue and secure with wire, ½ in (12mm) below the glued-on lace frill. Trim away excess wire.

7 Wrap the wider ribbon around the tip of the dowel (step 5) and over the wire (step 6). Form a loop from the narrower ribbon and glue this to the front of the parasol. Top with a bow made from the remaining ribbon.

PADDED ANGEL

MATERIALS

Decorative felt, 6 x 12in (15 x 30cm)
$\frac{1}{2}$ round shoulder pad, or cut pattern (see page 123)
from foam rubber, $\frac{1}{4}$in (6mm) thick
Fabric glue
Scissors
1 large wooden bead with large hole in one side
Acrylic paint
Small paintbrush
Scalloped scissors (optional)
Large needle and carpet thread
12in (30cm) gold metallic ricrac
1 large gold star (from an inexpensive tree garland)
Low temperature glue gun and glue sticks
1 small gold star (from a tree garland)
5in (12.5cm) gold cord
Small piece of gold-coloured, coiled scouring pad
10in (25cm) gold-edged, white satin ribbon, $\frac{1}{8}$in
(3mm) wide
1 tiny gold rosebud
10in (25cm) gold mesh wire ribbon, 1$\frac{1}{2}$in (4cm) wide
Cloth-covered wire

Padded angel and button wreath

1 Fold the piece of decorative felt in half, enclosing the shoulder pad or foam shape inside, with the straight edge of the shoulder pad against the fold. Apply a liberal amount of fabric glue around the curved edge of the shoulder pad and press the felt down firmly with your fingers to close. Run a thumbnail or closed scissors tip around the edge to ensure that the glue bonds well. Allow the glue to dry for 4 to 6 hours.

2 Using a small paintbrush, paint the large wooden bead with a base coat of flesh colour acrylic paint. Then paint the eyes using the round handle end of a paintbrush to form two dots. Paint two round circles for the cheeks.

3 Cut around the curved edge of the pad, through the glued portion to trim the excess felt. It is particularly effective if you use scalloped scissors or pinking shears.

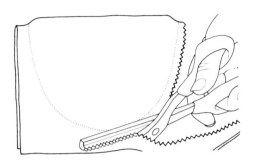

4 Fold the two corners towards the centre and overlap them slightly. Using a large heavy needle and carpet thread, secure the corners down with a few catching stitches, with a knot at the back.

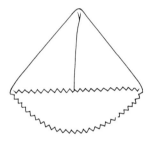

5 Glue the gold ricrac onto the felt about ½in (12mm) above the cut edge. Start in the front on one side, run it around the back to end up in front where you started. Cover the join of the two cut ends by gluing on the large star using the glue gun. Glue the small star over the knot at the back, arranging the trim in a pleasing manner.

6 Glue the painted head bead on the point at the top. Form a loop from the gold cord and glue it to the top of the head to make a hanging loop. Cover the glued end of the loop with pieces of scouring pad for cute hair curls. Trim where necessary.

7 Make a collar bow for the angel with the gold-edged ribbon and glue it under the chin of the head bead. Glue a rosebud to the centre of the bow.

8 Form a circle with mesh wire ribbon, overlapping the ends slightly. Wind wire around the middle of the loop to form a bow. Glue this to the centre of the back of the angel to form wings.

BUTTON WREATH

MATERIALS

Craft knife
Pair of compasses
Heavy gold mountboard
Gold acrylic paint
Small paintbrush
Low temperature glue gun and glue sticks
Assorted white buttons
Assorted gold buttons
15in (38cm) gold mesh wire ribbon, 1½in (4cm) wide
Small piece of florist's wire
5in (12.5cm) gold cord

1 Using a craft knife and a pair of compasses, cut a 4in (10cm) circle from the mountboard. Cut a 1¾in (4.5cm) hole in the centre. Paint the outer white edge of the mountboard circle with the gold paint.

2 Glue white buttons to the inner white side of the circle in a pleasing manner. Glue on a few gold buttons in between the white buttons to add some interest.

3 Form a circle with the mesh wire ribbon, overlapping the ends slightly. Wind florist's wire around the middle of the loop to form a bow. Set aside.

4 Form a loop from the gold cord and attach it to the top of the wreath to form the hanging loop. Glue the bow formed in step 3 over the knot of the hanging loop. Cover the wired centre of the bow with a small decorative button.

DOILY BASKET

MATERIALS

Crocheted doily (round or heart-shaped),
4in (10cm) wide
Fabric stiffener
Damp sponge
Cocktail stick
Aluminium foil
Small, round bottle, approximately 1in (2.5cm) in
diameter
4in (10cm) crocheted lace, ½in (12mm) wide
Low temperature glue gun and glue sticks
24in (60cm) burgundy satin ribbon, ¹⁄₁₆in (1.5mm) wide
1 medium folded ribbon rosebud
2 sprigs green moss
Gypsophila

1 Coat the doily on both sides with fabric stiffener, applying it with your fingers. Pat the doily well with the damp sponge to remove the excess stiffener. Use a cocktail stick to poke through the holes in the doily to clear them of the stiffener.

2 Wrap aluminium foil around a small round bottle. Wrap the doily around the bottle and allow to dry overnight.

3 Apply fabric stiffener to the crocheted lace with your fingers as in step 1. Allow the lace to dry flat.

4 To assemble the basket, glue each end of the flat lace to opposite sides of the doily basket base.

5 Make a 2½in (6.5cm) triple loop bow from the burgundy ribbon. Glue it to one side of the basket where the handle and basket meet. Glue a ribbon rosebud to the centre of the bow.

6 Fill the basket with green moss and scatter gypsophila over the top for extra interest.

DOILY HEART

MATERIALS

Papier mâché heart, 3in (7.5cm) wide
Gold metallic acrylic paint
Paintbrush
Crocheted doily, 6in (15cm) in diameter
Cloth-covered wire
24in (60cm) burgundy satin ribbon, ¹⁄₁₆in (1.5mm) wide
Low temperature glue gun and glue sticks
1 ribbon rose
Gold hanging cord (if necessary)

1 Paint the papier mâché heart with a coat of gold metallic acrylic paint and allow to dry.

2 Place the heart in the centre of the doily and gather up the edges of the doily neatly (see the diagram). Check to make sure the heart is centred and secure the doily edges by wrapping around with wire.

3 Arrange the gathers evenly to form a small lace circle. Lay the gathers back against the heart. Make a 2in (¾cm) wide bow from the burgundy ribbon and glue it just above the gathers. Glue a ribbon rose in the centre of the gathers.

4 If the papier mâché heart does not have a hanger attached, make one from a loop of gold cord. Pull the hanger through a gap in the doily at the top of the heart.

Opposite *Doily basket and doily heart*

PARCEL ORNAMENTS

MATERIALS

Stiff card

Pencil

Ruler

Scissors

Tacky glue

Decorative wrapping paper

Floristry ribbon, 2in (5cm) wide

Cord

1 Using the pattern given on page 124, draw out the box shapes on stiff card with a pencil and ruler. Cut out the box shapes. Score along the fold lines using a pair of scissors to make neater folds, and glue the small tabs to construct the box.

2 For each box cut out one piece of wrapping paper measuring 6 x 3in (15 x 7.5cm).

3 Starting in the centre of one side panel of the box, wrap the length of the paper around it until it slightly overlaps the other cut edge of the paper (this should be in the centre of the side panel, which can then be covered by ribbon). Glue the paper down to secure. When dry, fold the ends of the paper down in an envelope fashion. Glue to secure. Repeat with the other side.

4 Cut the ribbon into the following lengths: one piece 22in (55cm) long and one piece 8in (20cm) long. Tear each of these into eight strips (making each strip ¼in (6mm) wide). For each box you will need one strip 22in (55cm) long and ¼in (6mm) wide, and eight strips 8in (20cm) long and ¼in (6mm) wide.

5 Wrap the longer strip of ribbon around the box. Start by leaving approximately a 3–4in (7.5–10cm) tail. After wrapping it around once and returning to the beginning, twist the ribbon and wrap it around the other side. Take the remaining loose end of ribbon and wrap it under the twist of ribbon at the top and pull it through. Pull it taut and tie once if you wish.

6 Tie the shorter strips of ribbon tightly onto the top of the box. Curl the ribbon strips by holding one strip at a time, as close to the central knot as possible, between the thumb and sharp edge of the scissors. Pull firmly to

the end to form a curl. Repeat, holding more tightly, if a tighter curl is preferred. Curl the ends of ribbon which formed the knot.

7 Cut a 10in (25cm) length of cord. Carefully slip one cut end under the central knot holding the curls. Pull through to the other side. Tie the two ends of the cord in a tight reef knot. Trim the ends if necessary and gently pull the loop around so that the knot slides under the central ribbon knot, hidden under the ribbon curls.

Parcel ornaments (see page 97) and miniature crackers

MINIATURE CRACKERS

MATERIALS

Coloured foil paper, $6^{1}/_{2}$ x 4in (16.5 x 10cm)

Stiff card, 2 x $3^{3}/_{4}$in (5 x 9.5cm)

Tacky glue

2 formers (plastic piping, 1in (2.5cm) in diameter), 6in
(15cm) long and 4in (10cm) long

Cloth

Waxed cord

Floristry ribbon

Scissors

*As these crackers are for decorative purposes only, you
will not need snaps, mottoes or toys to stuff inside.*

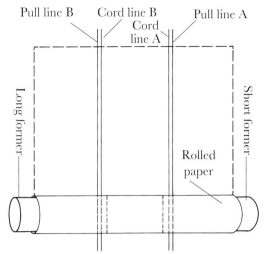

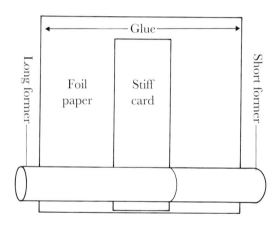

1 Place the foil paper, coloured side down, onto the work surface. Place the stiff card in the centre of the foil, along the bottom edge. Spread glue along the top edge of the foil paper (see the diagram).

2 Place the long former horizontally on the bottom left and the short former horizontally on the bottom right of the foil, butting the ends of the formers along the right-hand edge of the stiff card. Tightly roll the foil around the formers, holding the formers together, until you have rolled up the foil to reach the glue. Continue to roll the foil over the glued edge. Wipe away any excess glue with a cloth and allow to dry.

3 Taking the short former on the right, pull it about $^{1}/_{4}$in (6mm) away from the right-hand edge of the stiff card (called 'pull line A' on the diagram). Wrap the waxed cord twice around the foil, centrally between the right-hand edge of the stiff card and the left-hand edge of the short former (called 'cord line A' on the diagram).

4 Holding the two ends of the waxed cord, pull them in opposite directions. This will cause the cord to form a crease at the edge of the stiff card. Push the short former back against the long former and the stiff card to shape the cracker. Remove the waxed cord, then remove the short former.

5 Take the long tube on the left and pull it to 'pull line B'. Wrap the cord twice around the foil at 'cord line B'. Pull the cord tightly as in step 4. To shape the cracker, gently push the long former tube back against the stiff card. Remove the cord and former.

6 Decorate the cracker with ribbon, curling it by running a scissor blade along its length, and tying it in the creased sides of the cracker.

ICICLES

MATERIALS

(per icicle)

Long-nosed pliers

4in (10cm) white chenille stem (12in (30cm) stem cut into thirds)

Cord or strong thread (for hanging loop)

6 crystal sunburst beads, 12mm

6 crystal sunburst beads, 10mm

3 crystal faceted beads, 8mm

3 crystal faceted beads, 6mm

2 crystal faceted beads, 4mm

Tacky glue

Wire cutters or strong scissors (for cutting wire)

Ribbon rose, ribbon bow and lace bow for decoration (optional)

1 Using pliers, form a small tight loop at one end of the chenille stem. Thread cord or strong thread through the loop and tie this in a knot for the hanging loop.

2 Thread beads onto the chenille stem in the following order: 6 x sunburst beads, 12mm; 6 x sunburst beads, 10mm; 3 x faceted beads, 8mm; 3 x faceted beads, 6mm; 1 x faceted bead, 4mm. Push them up to the looped end and twist until they slot together. The fit must be tight; however, if there is any difficulty pushing the beads onto the chenille stem, trim away some bristles along the wire.

3 Dab glue on the end of the chenille stem; thread on the last 4mm faceted bead. Rotate the bead so that the glue spreads around. Wipe away excess glue. Trim any excess chenille stem with wire cutters or scissors.

4 Decorate the icicle as desired. Here a ribbon rose has been glued over a satin ribbon bow and lace bow for a Victorian flavour.

WINTER WONDERLAND

MATERIALS

Tacky glue

16in (40cm) gold braided metallic cord, $\frac{1}{32}$in (0.75mm) wide

2 crystal squatty bicone beads, 18 x 16mm

2 crystal squatty bicone beads, 13 x 10mm

2 crystal elongated bicone beads, 13 x 6mm

2 crystal faceted round beads, 8mm

2 crystal faceted round beads, 10mm

10 gold-washed floral rondelle beads, 6mm

2 gold-washed round beads, 4mm

Scissors

14in (35cm) gold glitter ribbon, $\frac{5}{8}$in (1.5cm) wide

1 Dab glue on both ends of the cord to keep them from unravelling while stringing on the beads. Tie an overhand knot at one end of the cord. String on the beads as shown.

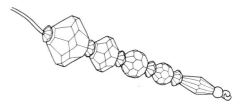

2 String on step 1 beads in reverse order. Tie an overhand knot in the other end of the cord. Dab glue on both knots. When it has dried, trim away the cord ends close to the knots. Slide the two sets of beads to the opposite ends of the cord, as shown.

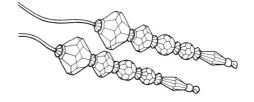

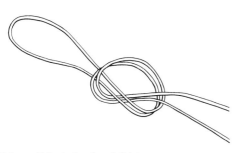

Winter Wonderland and Icicles

3 Fold the cord so that one icicle is approximately 1in (12mm) lower than the other. Tie an overhand knot (left) 1½in (4cm) from the fold, forming a loop to hang on the tree.

4 Tie a bow with the gold ribbon over the top of the overhand knot.

Table Setting

Victorians were great home lovers and the Christmas festivities provided them with an opportunity to celebrate with friends and family. Special treats, which were only served once a year or on very rare occasions, were lavishly provided to tempt every palate. And, to frame this array of culinary delights, the Christmas table setting was made extra special with the rich array of home-made garlands and decorations.

This table is hung with a lacy-covered tablecloth. Table runners in rich burgundy provide the background to the table service. The decorative theme is set by the two-tiered centrepiece of golden wicker, greenery, pine cones and fruit, flanked by the rosy glow of warm candlelight, while serviette rings of ribbon, adorned with a miniature wicker wreath to co-ordinate with the centrepiece, are decorated with a profusion of satin ribbons, roses and pearls.

Serviette rings, above (see page 105) and table centrepiece, right (see page 104)

TABLE CENTREPIECE

MATERIALS

Wicker wreath, 12in (30cm) in diameter

Wicker wreath, 9in (22.5cm) in diameter

Gold aerosol paint

Scissors

5yd (4.4m) gold-edged wine moiré ribbon, 1in (2.5cm) wide

Low temperature glue gun and glue sticks

1 companion stand (for fireplace tools) without the tools

Florist's wire

4yd (3.6m) gold-edged wine moiré ribbon, 1½in (4cm) wide

Floral sprays for decoration

1 Spray the two wicker wreaths with gold paint in a well-ventilated area. Leave to dry.

2 Cut four pieces of the narrower ribbon, each 30in (75cm) long. Wrap them, one at a time, and an equal distance apart, around the larger wreath and tie the ends in a knot. Glue the knot underneath the wreath, out of sight.

3 Place the larger wreath over the companion stand and loop the ribbon onto the hooks at the top and secure.

4 Repeat step 2 with the smaller wreath and four pieces of ribbon each 18½in (46.5cm) long. Place the small wreath over the companion stand so that it hangs just above the larger wreath. Thread a piece of florist's wire through the ribbon loops and attach them to the hooks on the companion.

5 Using the wider ribbon, make four bows. Attach them to the ribbon loops around the smaller wicker wreath.

6 Decorate the wreaths with floral sprays and the remaining ribbon.

TABLE RUNNER

MATERIALS
(for one lengthwise and one widthwise runner)

2¼yd (2m) fabric

Scissors

Tape measure

Pins

4 tassels

11½yd (10m) insertion cord

Needle and cotton

1 For the lengthwise runner, cut two pieces of fabric, each measuring 78 x 13½in (195 x 34cm). Fold in half along its length and measure 8in (20cm) from both corners of the folded edge across to the outside edge to form the angle of the point at each end (see diagram). Cut along this line at both ends.

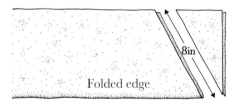

2 Unfold the fabric and pin a tassel to each of the longest points on the right side of one piece of fabric. Pin it with the fringed edge facing away from the cut edge. Baste the insertion cord around the edge of the right side of the same runner piece, ¼in (6mm) from the edge, over the end of the tassel.

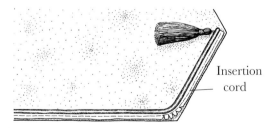

3 Place the two pieces of the table runner together, with right sides facing, and stitch around the outside edge next to the cord, leaving a ¼in (6mm) seam allowance. Leave an 8in

(20cm) opening for turning. Clip the corners and turn the runner the right way out. Hand-stitch the opening closed. Press.

4 To make the widthwise runner, cut two pieces of fabric, each measuring 52 x 13½in (130 x 34cm). Repeat steps 1 to 3.

SERVIETTE RINGS

MATERIALS

(for one serviette ring)

Small wicker wreath, 2in (5cm) in diameter

Gold acrosol paint

Scissors

Card tube (from kitchen roll)

Tacky glue

14in (35cm) gold-edged wine moiré ribbon, 1½in (4cm) wide

19in (47.5cm) cream or ivory gathered lace, ½in (12mm) wide

8in (20cm) fused pearls

7 ribbon rosebuds

1 Spray the wicker wreath with gold paint in a well-ventilated area. Allow to dry.

2 Cut a 1½in (4cm) wide section from the card tube. Glue ribbon over the outside of the card tube. Glue lace around both inside edges of the card tube. Glue ribbon around the inside of the card tube, covering the edge of lace glued there.

3 Wrap fused pearls around the wreath, and secure with glue. Glue the remaining lace around the outside edge of the wicker wreath.

4 Glue the wreath to the ribbon-covered card tube. Decorate with ribbon rosebuds, gluing them down to secure.

Table runner and serviette rings

Room Decorations

The Victorians spent a great deal of time preparing their homes for the Christmas celebrations. They lavishly adorned every conceivable corner with garlands, bows and sprays of ivy, holly or evergreens. Fragrant foliage was draped over picture frames, along bannisters and balustrades, and around fireplace mantelpieces. Wreaths could be found hung on doors or behind window panes. The Victorian shops did not have a wide selection of ready-made seasonal items to purchase as we have today. Therefore, many natural elements found in the meadows and woodlands were used among a backdrop of fresh, rich greenery; flowers, pine cones, berries and fruit were all used to create colourful displays.

You too can add a touch of Victorian charm to your Christmas decorations by making your own swags to hang over the fireplace, picture frames or balustrades. Invite other members of the family to get involved and share the fun of creative crafting, as enjoyed by our Victorian ancestors.

VICTORIAN SWAG

Artificial garlands are easily available in most Christmas decoration departments. They can be decorated in many creative ways to complement other ornaments in the room setting. By making your own swag, whether it is from fresh, dried or preserved greenery, you can add greater variety of colour, texture and fullness to the garland.

If you want a garland that can be used year after year, use artificial greenery for the base and tuck in a few fresh branches here and there. Dried or preserved greenery gives the more realistic look of a fresh garland, and has the advantage that it can be used on more than one occasion.

Making swags from fresh foliage is both quick and easy. Hand-made garlands have a much fuller shape and, in addition to the dramatic backdrop for other decorations in the room, they provide a fragrance which sets the seasonal ambience.

MATERIALS

Rope or thick cord
Fresh, dried or preserved greenery
Secateurs
20–22 gauge florist's or craft wire

1 Form a small loop at one end of the rope and tie a knot. Form a loop at the other end of the rope, once you have determined the desired length of the swag, taking into account any draping.

around the already wired end of the bunch, with the loose tips overlapping the loop. Wire one bunch at the back and the remaining two in front.

3 Wire a second grouping of three bunches around the rope, moving a little further along the rope so that the greenery covers the wire from the previous foliage. Continue adding bunches of wired foliage until you reach the end of the rope.

4 Turn some greenery bunches to lie in the opposite direction and wire them between the bunches already placed.

5 Position the garland in place and decorate.

2 Cut the greenery into small sprigs. Wire up bunches of greenery with three small sprigs per bunch. Wire three bunches of greenery to the end rope. Wrap the wire

CHAPTER 7

A Country Theme

IN TODAY'S MODERN WORLD, commercialism threatens to overcome every aspect of our lives. With our country theme I have looked towards nature for a less artificial approach to the decoration of tree and home.

By observing the profusion of natural materials that can be found in the woods and fields, along the highways and riverbanks, you too can create your own country-style decorations to imitate the glorious wealth of beauty found in nature. The ingredients for this theme can be collected throughout the year, with each season providing its own contribution.

The same choice of nature's goodies are used throughout the home, from the welcoming wreath, the Christmas tree and swag, to the festive table. Why not use a family outing to give each member the opportunity of contributing to the seasonal decorations? With little expense and lots of creative satisfaction, you can build on your country theme from one year to the next.

Tree Decorations

On the country Christmas tree I have used bows made from hessian ribbon to hold up the cocoa rope swag. The tree is lit by the use of tiny white tree lights, so the honeycomb candles in rope-covered pots are for decoration only. Small rose-filled terracotta pots and nut baskets peek out among the collection of cinnamon stick bundles, preserved oranges, pine cones, colourful fabric hearts and gilded biscuits. The whole array is guarded by a hessian tree-top angel and her band of heavenly colleagues.

HANGING CANDLES

MATERIALS
Scissors
40in (1m) cocoa rope (for each hanging candle)
Low temperature glue gun and glue sticks
Terracotta pots, 1½in (4cm) high and 1¾in (4.5cm) in diameter
Honeycomb candles, 4in (10cm) high and ¾in (2cm) in diameter
Flat moss

1 Cut a 10½in (26cm) piece of cocoa rope and form it into a loop so that the ends lie side by side (not end to end). Glue the ends of the rope loop to the inside of a terracotta pot.

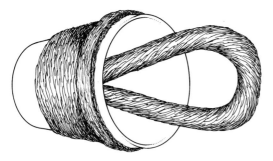

2 Coil the remaining rope around the outside of the terracotta pot, gluing it in place with the glue gun.

3 Glue the candle in the centre of the pot and stuff flat moss around it to hold it in place. Repeat to make as many hanging candles as you like.

CAUTION: These candles are for decoration only. Lit candles can be a serious fire hazard on the tree.

TERRACOTTA POTS WITH ROSES

MATERIALS
90-gauge wire
Terracotta pots, 1½in (4cm) high and 1¾in (4.5cm) in diameter
Dry florist's foam
Flat moss
Dried rosebuds (3 per pot)

1 Bend a 12in (30cm) piece of wire in half. Thread one half of the wire up through the hole at the bottom of a terracotta pot to the lip at the top of the pot. The other half of the wire should remain on the outside of the terracotta pot.

2 Twist the two ends of the folded wire together as neatly as possible. This wire can then be used to attach the completed pot to the tree.

3 Pack the inside of the terracotta pot with dry florist's foam and cover the top of the foam with flat moss.

Hanging candles, terracotta pots with roses and preserved orange slices (see page 112)

4 Poke a 6in (15cm) wire through the bottom of a rosebud, about ³⁄₈in (4mm) from the stem. Twist the ends of the wire together. Poke three wired rosebuds into each pot.

PRESERVED ORANGE SLICES

MATERIALS

Fruit knife

Fresh, firm oranges

Paper towels

Low temperature glue gun and glue sticks

Raffia

1 Slice the oranges about ¼in (6mm) thick. Put two layers of paper towels in a microwave-proof dish. Place the slices of two oranges at a time on top of the paper towels.

2 Bake the orange slices in a microwave oven on high for about 6 to 10 minutes until the slices turn very bright yellow. The length of time will vary, depending on how juicy the oranges are and the strength of the oven. When you remove the orange slices, they will be sticky and spongy to the touch and the paper towels will be saturated. You may need to experiment with this stage.

3 Place the orange slices in a pre-heated oven on the lowest possible setting and bake for about 45 minutes. Watch the oranges carefully and test them regularly as the length of time can vary according to the texture of the orange, the type of oven and the air humidity.

4 To assemble the ornaments, take three slices and cut two of them in half. Glue the four halves on each side of the remaining whole slice at a 45° angle (see the diagram).

Country angel and country hearts (see page 114)

5 Poke a hole in the top of one end of the whole orange slice, thread through a piece of raffia and knot it to form a hanging loop.

COUNTRY ANGEL

MATERIALS

These amounts are for making the tree-top angel.
You can make smaller angel tree ornaments by reducing the materi-
als proportionately.

1 wooden head bead, 1¾in (4.5cm) long
Acrylic paints
Small paintbrush
Cotton swab
Cosmetic powder blusher
Fusible adhesive
Hessian fabric, 12in (30cm) square
Thin card
Tracing paper
Pencil
Scissors
Ruler
Low temperature glue gun and glue sticks
Clothes peg
Spanish moss
28-gauge gold-coloured wire
Raffia
Small beads
18in (45cm) hessian ribbon

1 Paint the wooden head bead with flesh colour acrylic paint. When dry, paint black

eyes using the rounded end of the brush handle. Add a twinkle to her eyes by painting a tiny dot in the outer corner of each eye. Dab a cotton swab in cosmetic powder blusher, then dab it on the bead to form cheeks.

2 Following the manufacturer's instructions, fuse the hessian fabric to one side of the thin card using fusible adhesive. Trace the pattern (see page 123) on the card side and cut out. Cut out two 3in (7.5cm) squares of hessian.

3 To make the dress/body, form the scalloped card and fabric piece into a cone shape by lining up the last scallop on each cut end. Glue the edges together and peg until dry.

4 Form the sleeves/arms by rolling each 3in (7.5cm) square of hessian fabric into a cone shape by overlapping and gluing the opposite corners. Rolling the card around a pencil first makes them easier to form.

5 Glue the sleeves to the sides of the larger cone by lining them up; the small point of the arms should be at the top and the seam should be along the edge to be glued.

6 Glue the wooden head bead over the point of the large cone. Glue Spanish moss to the back of the head bead to form hair. Make a circular halo with 4in (10cm) of wire, leaving ½in (12mm) at each end free. Twist the ends together and bend at right angles to the circle. Glue this inside the back of the hair.

7 Tie a small raffia bow and glue this under the head bead (chin) at the front. Glue a few small beads down from the bow to create the illusion of buttons.

8 Fold the cut ends of the hessian ribbon to the centre, overlapping them slightly. Wrap wire around the centre to form a large bow. Glue this to the angel's back for the wings.

COUNTRY HEARTS

MATERIALS

Pinking shears or straight-edged scissors

Scraps of cotton fabric (small Christmas print)

Wadding

Needle and thread

Raffia

Fabric glue

1 Using the pattern given on page 122, cut out at least two hearts from the same cotton fabric. Use either pinking shears for a serrated edge, or straight-edged scissors for a frayed edge. Cut out a piece of wadding $\frac{1}{4}$in (6mm) smaller than the pattern.

2 With wrong sides together, hand-stitch the two fabric hearts together, $\frac{1}{4}$in (6mm) from the cut edge, leaving a small opening.

3 Insert the piece of wadding through the opening and stitch the opening to close.

4 Make a loop with a length of raffia. Glue this to the front of the heart where it dips at the top. Tie a small raffia bow and glue this over the cut ends of the raffia loop. Repeat the steps to make further country hearts.

MINIATURE BASKET OF NUTS

MATERIALS

Scissors

Cocoa rope

Low temperature glue gun and glue sticks

Small rectangular basket

Dry florist's foam

Flat moss

Mixture of nuts and small cones

1 Cut a 4in (10cm) piece of cocoa rope and glue each end to the opposite sides of the inside of the basket.

2 Stuff the basket with florist's foam. Then cover the outside edges of the basket and a little of the florist's foam with flat moss.

3 Glue nuts and small cones over the florist's foam, building up layers which spill over the sides of the basket, as shown opposite.

CHRISTMAS COOKIES

MATERIALS

Mixing bowl

Wooden spoon

4oz (125g) butter

6oz (185g/ $\frac{2}{3}$ cup) icing sugar

1 egg yolk

2 teaspoons vanilla essence

Sieve

8oz (250g/2 cups) plain flour

Rolling pin

Baking parchment

Biscuit cutters

Skewer

Gold aerosol paint

Raffia

1 Pre-heat the oven to 160°C (325°F/Gas Mark 3). In a mixing bowl, beat together the butter, sugar, egg yolk and vanilla essence until the mixture is creamy and light. Gradually sift in the flour and mix to a soft dough.

2 Roll out the dough between sheets of baking parchment until it is about $\frac{1}{4}$in (6mm) thick. Cut the dough into varying shapes using biscuit cutters.

3 Using a skewer or similar instrument, poke a hole in each cookie. It should be large enough to thread raffia through.

4 Bake the cookies for 20 minutes on the top shelf of the oven. Allow to cool.

CAUTION: These cookies are for decoration only and should not be eaten, so hang them out of reach of very young children.

Christmas cookies, preserved orange slices and miniature baskets of nuts

5 In a well-ventilated area, spray both the front and back of the cookies with a light coat of gold aerosol paint. Leave to dry.

6 When the cookies are completely dry, thread a 10in (25cm) piece of raffia through cookie and tie the ends together to form a hanging loop.

Room Decorations

Extend the festive country theme throughout your home by making one of the projects in this section. The elaborate country Christmas swag, made using an attractive selection of dried and preserved seed heads, cones and fruit, would look wonderful draped above a mantelpiece. Alternatively, you can make a resplendent wreath for the front door using an abundance of natural ingredients, including oranges, lemons, cinnamon and chillies. When you look at nature's harvest, you will find a wealth of materials you can plunder for use in room decorations.

COUNTRY CHRISTMAS SWAG

MATERIALS

7ft (2.2m) wire-edged ribbon
90-gauge florist's wire
Low temperature glue gun and glue sticks
Dried rosebuds or nuts
Pre-made evergreen swag (see pages 106-107)
Dried artichokes
Gold aerosol paint
Cinnamon sticks
Raffia
Artificial pomegranates
Poppy heads
Freeze-dried whole oranges
Preserved Orange Slices (see page 112)
Assorted cones (eg, Wiltonian, pine, larch, Cedar of Lebanon)
Chillies
Country Hearts made from hessian (see page 114)

1 Form two large bows using 44in (1.1m) of wire-edged ribbon for each bow. Do not tie the bows; hold them in place by wrapping wire around the centre. Glue a cluster of nuts to the centre of each, covering the wire. Wire one bow into each corner of the pre-made evergreen swag.

2 In a well-ventilated area, lightly gild the dried artichokes with gold aerosol paint. When dry, twist wire around the stem of each artichoke and attach them to the swag.

3 Make up the cinnamon stick bunches by tying three or four sticks together with raffia. Wrap a 10in (25cm) piece of wire around the raffia at the back of the bundle. Twist the ends together and use this to attach the bunch to the swag.

4 Poke a hole in one end of each pomegranate. Taking each pomegranate in turn, glue one end of a piece of wire in the hole. To attach the pomegranate to the swag, twist the wire end into the swag.

5 Using wire, tie together seven poppy heads into a bunch. Cover the wire with raffia. Use the wire to attach the bunch to the swag.

6 Poke a piece of wire through one end of the freeze-dried whole oranges and orange

Opposite Country Christmas swag

116

slices in turn. Wire them together in groups, then attach them to the swag with wire.

7 Fill in the gaps and spaces on the swag by wiring on groups of assorted cones and chillies (in bunches of five), together with country hearts.

COUNTRY CHRISTMAS DOOR WREATH

MATERIALS

Low temperature glue gun and glue sticks
90-gauge wire, cut into 12in (30cm) lengths
Twigs
Moss-covered wreath, 16in (40cm) in diameter
Raffia
6 freeze-dried oranges
12 Preserved Orange Slices (see page 112)
24 poppy heads
4 artificial pomegranates
6 lotus heads
20 cinnamon sticks
Assorted pods, as available (I used rose de tefé and brachychiton)
Assorted cones
Dried chillies

1 Glue or wire small twigs to the back of the moss-covered wreath so that they protrude around the outside edge of the wreath.

2 Take a handful of long raffia strands and tie the strands into an 8in (20cm) bow (when measured across the width of the loops). Glue the bow to the top of the wreath.

3 Using the glue gun, attach four groups of whole preserved oranges and orange slices to the wreath. I have made two groups of one freeze-dried orange and three preserved slices;

the remaining two groups each have two whole oranges and three preserved slices.

4 Prepare three bunches of eight poppy heads by wiring them together. Position and wire them to the wreath.

5 Poke a hole in one end of each pomegranate and glue in one end of wire. Twist two pomegranate wires together and wire to the wreath.

6 Poke a wire through the bottom end of the lotus heads. Bring the wire ends together and twist. Make two groups of lotus heads by wiring three heads together for each group. Wire the groups to the wreath.

7 Make five cinnamon stick bundles by tying four or more sticks together with raffia. Glue these to the wreath.

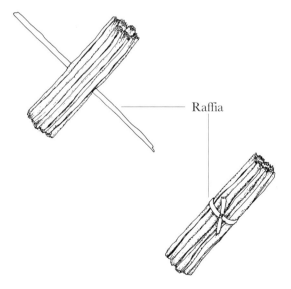

Raffia

8 Fill in the remaining gaps on the wreath by gluing into place various assorted pods, cones and bunches of chillies.

Opposite *Country Christmas door wreath*

Table Setting

Study the lush abundance of fruit rich with nature's autumnal bounty overflowing from the candle basket of our table centrepiece. It joins the mulled wine and homemade mince pies in anticipation of the feast ahead, while serviette rings are quickly put together using cinnamon stick bundles decorated with preserved orange slices, dried rosebuds and little cones.

TABLE CENTREPIECE

MATERIALS

Three-candle basket
Dry florist's foam
Green flat moss
90-gauge wire
Green preserved beech
Rustic-coloured preserved tree ivy with berries
Assorted cones of various sizes (eg, Wiltonian, pine, larch, Cedar of Lebanon)
3–5 lotus heads
16 poppy heads
6 protea buds
Preserved Orange Slices (see page 112)
Low temperature glue gun and glue sticks
3 freeze-dried whole oranges
3 freeze-dried whole lemons
3 mock apples
6 mock damsons
3 artificial pomegranates
3 rose de tefé or similar pods
Dried chillies
Cinnamon sticks
Raffia
3 cream candles, 12in (30cm) long and 1in (2.5cm) in diameter

1 Fill the centre of the candle basket with florist's foam and cover with green flat moss.

2 Wire together six bunches of green beech and poke them into the florist's foam. Spread them evenly over the centre of the basket.

3 Wire together three bunches of tree ivy with berries and poke these into the florist's foam, spreading them evenly between the beech.

4 Wire together six groups of various sizes and types of cone. To wire a cone, take a 10in (25cm) piece of wire and wrap it around the bottom (wider) edge of the cone through the scales. Bring the two wires together and twist.

5 Poke a 10in (25cm) wire through the bottom end of the lotus heads. Bring the wire ends together and twist. Spread three to five of these lotus heads evenly throughout the arrangement.

6 Wire poppy heads into four groups of between three and five heads, and poke them into the florist's foam around the arrangement. Position six protea buds individually around the arrangement.

7 Wire together three groups of preserved orange slices; wire these into the arrangement. Glue three freeze-dried whole oranges and three freeze-dried whole lemons in the arrangement.

8 Add three mock apples and three groups of two mock damsons which have been wired together. Poke three wired artificial pomegranates into the arrangement.

CAUTION: Burning candles should never be left unattended.

Table centrepiece

9 Fill in any gaps with rose de tefé or similar pods and chillies. Finish off the centre of the arrangement with small bunches of cinnamon sticks tied together with raffia. Place the candles into the basket rings and pack with moss.

121

Templates

ALL TEMPLATES are actual size, unless otherwise stated. When tracing half-templates, flip the tracing paper to trace the mirror image for the other half.

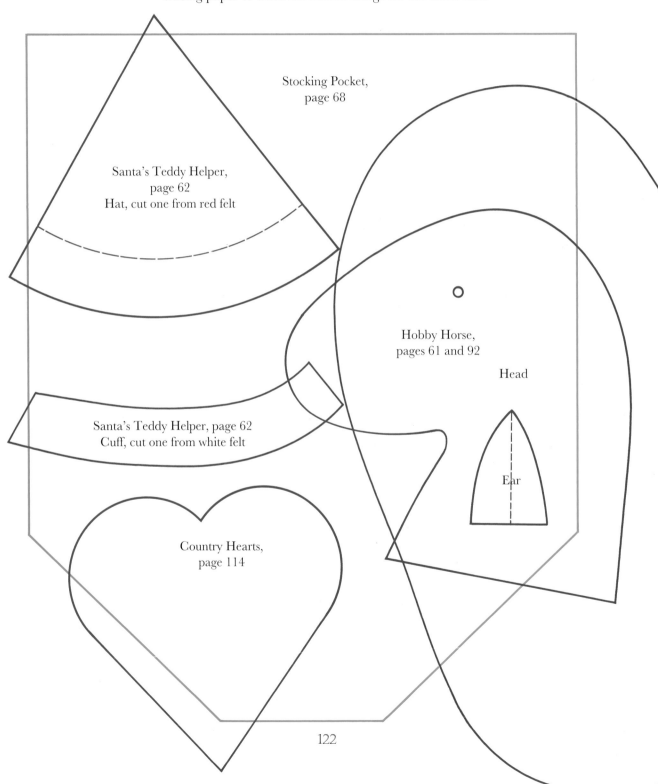

Stocking Pocket,
page 68

Santa's Teddy Helper,
page 62
Hat, cut one from red felt

Hobby Horse,
pages 61 and 92

Head

Santa's Teddy Helper, page 62
Cuff, cut one from white felt

Ear

Country Hearts,
page 114

122

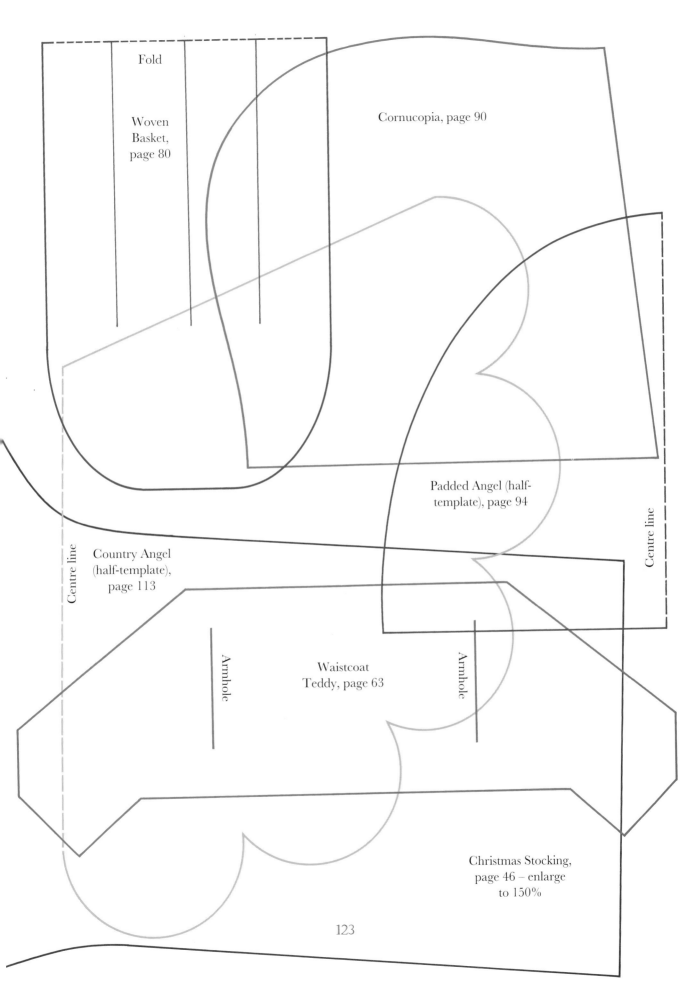

Fold

Woven
Basket,
page 80

Cornucopia, page 90

Padded Angel (half-
template), page 94

Centre line

Country Angel
(half-template),
page 113

Centre line

Armhole

Waistcoat
Teddy, page 63

Armhole

Christmas Stocking,
page 46 – enlarge
to 150%

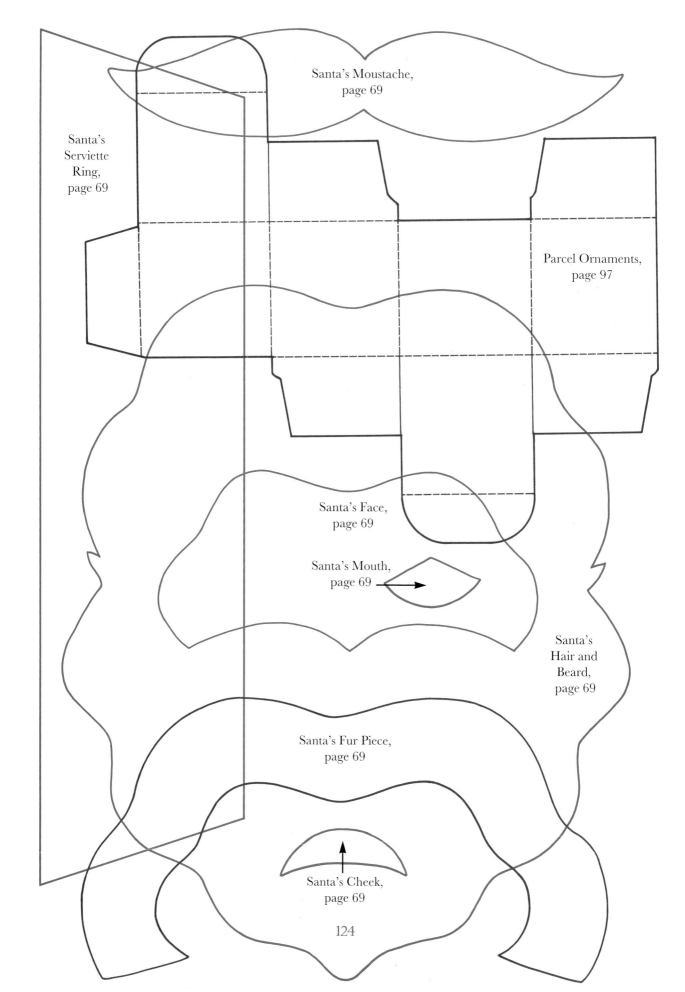

Santa's Moustache,
page 69

Santa's
Serviette
Ring,
page 69

Parcel Ornaments,
page 97

Santa's Face,
page 69

Santa's Mouth,
page 69

Santa's
Hair and
Beard,
page 69

Santa's Fur Piece,
page 69

Santa's Cheek,
page 69

Beaded Table Linen,
page 32

Acknowledgements

I would like to say a very special thank you to the following for all their help in completing this book:

Debbie Vertrees for designing and making decorations. Debbie not only made up the projects from designs I had in mind, but she also contributed ideas and designs of her own, particularly in the Tartan, Toyland and Victorian chapters.

Marion Wright for making decorations, and designing and dressing trees. Marion was my faithful assistant without whom this book would have taken another four years! She made samples and designs to specification and spent early mornings and late nights not only completing the decorations but also helping to decorate the trees, swags and tables.

Laila Paulsen-Becjac and **Kari Paulsen** for making projects and advising on the Scandinavian chapter. Kari gave me the idea of including a Scandinavian theme with her wonderful stories of Christmas in Norway and the fascinating decorations she had in her home every Christmas. Laila helped to source materials and collected information as well as translating, making up many of the various projects and designing the little *Julenisser*.

Bitte Kendal for advising on the Scandinavian chapter. Bitte spent hours telling me all about her early memories of the Christmas festivities from her childhood in Denmark, giving me ideas and background for the Scandinavian chapter.

Nancy Godsmark for making stiffened bows. Nancy is the best 'Stiffy' bow maker I know. She is responsible for making the projects with the gorgeous 'Stiffy' bows in the Tartan chapter.

Liz Davies and **Diane Mutkin** for designing and preparing projects in the Country chapter. Liz and Diane have a very special and unique talent which corresponded with my idea of a country Christmas theme.

Janet Cooper, Anne Flynn, Carol Nelson and Kathy Sanders for making decorations for the tree.

Tina Guillory for finding the most wonderful photography locations. She was a most helpful and encouraging stylist during the hectic and difficult photography sessions.

Caroline Arber took the most wonderful photographs. Her attention to detail and artistic talent has made the photography in this book superb.

Heather Dewhurst, who so patiently edited my many words and diagrams to make them into something quite wonderful!

I would like to thank the following companies for allowing us to use their products:

The Beadery supplied beads and gemstones and allowed us to use their 'Icicles' and 'Winter Wonderland' designs (available in kit form) in the Victorian chapter.

Creative Beadcraft Ltd provided the beads, pearls, sequins, filigree findings and braids for the pincraft ornaments and other decorations throughout the book.

Newey Goodman Ltd supplied the pins for the pincraft ornaments.

CM Offray & Son Ltd supplied all the ribbons used throughout the book.

Panduro Hobby kindly provided the materials for the Scandinavian chapter.

Plaid Enterprises for use of 'Folkart' acrylic and aerosol paints; 'Mod Podge' water-based glaze; 'Stiffy' fabric stiffener; 'Paper Capers' paper ribbon; 'Fashion Fabric Paint'; 'Shaper Paper' wire-edged paper ribbon.

Porth Innovations Ltd provided the artificial trees used in the Step by Step and Colour Theme chapters (sometimes at very short notice).

Rita Snelling at **Rainbow Ribbons** supplied the Bonbonniere for the Colour Themes table setting.

ThermOWeb for providing the fusible adhesive.

The rocking horse in our Toyland Christmas Tree photograph is a medium-sized FH Ayres horse on a safety stand. It is a faithful reproduction of a Victorian horse and is hand-stippled and with horse hair mane and tail and leather tack. Lent by **Stevenson Bros**, The Workshops, Ashford Road, Bethersden, Kent N26 3PA (Tel: 01233 820363)

All tree lights were kindly provided by **Noma Lites** and are available from all good department stores and garden centres.

All glassware, cutlery and china were very kindly loaned by **Aldis Superstores** of Fakenham, Norwich (Tel: 01328-855327), who also supplied carpets, furniture and linen.

The tree in the Victorian chapter was lent by **Fakenham Garden Centre** of Norfolk.

The bears in the Toyland chapter photographs were lent by **The Bear Shop** at both 18 Elm Hill, Norwich (Tel: 01603 766866) and 3 Sir Isaacs Walk, Colchester, Essex (Tel: 01206 577345).

Suppliers

The Beadery
PO Box 178, 105 Canonchet Road, Hope Valley, RI 02832 USA
Creative Beadcraft Ltd and W. Williams & Son Ltd distribute Beadery products in the UK.
Manufacturer of quality plastic beads and boxes

DIY Crackers
85 Princes Street, Southend, Essex SS1 1PT
Supplier of cracker materials (mail order)

Kinetic Needlecraft
10 The Pines, Broad Street, Guildford, Surrey GU3 3BH
Wholesaler of Christmas print fabrics

CM Offray & Son Ltd
Fir Tree Place, Church Road, Ashford, Middlesex TW15 2PH
Ribbon manufacturer

Panduro Hobby
Westway House, Transport Avenue, Brentford, Middlesex TW8 9HF
Distributor of general craft materials, (mail order, retail and wholesale)

Plaid Enterprises Inc
1649 International Blvd, PO Box 7600, Norcross, GA 300091-7600 USA
(W Williams & Son Ltd is the UK distributor of Plaid products)
Manufacturer of craft products such as: 'Folkart' acrylic paint and aerosol paint; 'Mod Podge' water-based glaze; 'Stiffy' fabric stiffener; 'Paper Capers' paper ribbon; 'Fashion Fabric Paint'; 'Shaper Paper' wire-edged paper ribbon, and publications

Porth Innovations Ltd
Cae Mawr Industrial Estate, Treorchy, Rhondda, Mid Glamorgan CF42 6EJ Manufacturer of Christmas trees, lights, ornaments and wholesale distributor of general craft supplies.

St Louis Trimming Inc
5040 Arsenal Street, St Louis, MO 63139 USA
(W Williams & Son Ltd is the UK distributor of St Louis Trimming laces)
Manufacturer of laces and trims

ThermOWeb
770 Glenn Avenue, Wheeling, IL 60090 USA
(W Williams & Son Ltd is the UK distributor of ThermOWeb products)
Manufacturer of Heat N Bond fusible adhesives.

Village Fabrics
PO Box 43, Wallingford, Oxfordshire OX10 9DF
Wholesaler and mail order of Christmas print fabrics

Weycraft
Wey Adhesives Ltd, PO Box 49, Godalming, Surrey GU8 5XY
Wholesale distributor of low temperature glue guns and glue sticks

W Williams & Son Ltd
Regent House, 1 Thane Villas, London N7 7PH
Wholesale distributor of craft products

Creative Beadcraft Ltd
Denmark Works, Sheepcote Dell Road, Beamond End, Buckinghamshire HP7 0RX
Wholesale and retail mail order of beads and trims

Index